M000112401

D1197754

INVESTING

ON YOUR OWN

TWO WHEELS

HOW BALANCED RISK & REWARD

FOSTER FINANCIAL FORTUNE

J. LAWRENCE BIXBY

Library of Congress Cataloging-in-Publication Data

Bixby, J. Lawrence

Investing On Your Own Two Wheels - How Balanced Risk & Reward Foster Financial Fortune / J. Lawrence Bixby

ISBN 978-0-578-87207-0 (paperback)

  1. Investing 2. Wealth Management 3. Analysis & Trading Strategies

To Willard and Jeanne - I walked Ivy League halls because of you. I remain eternally grateful.

To Zuzana - for reminding me how emotional it can be to start investing in stocks

To Nicki J - for making what I first drafted better for as long as you could stand it

To Kurt - for asking about things so obvious to me I should mention them to readers

To Danielle - for challenging me to reconsider the entire book from the outside in

To Steve - for keeping me honest throughout the book from the inside out

To investors not quite sure where to start -

   I still remember standing in your shoes, but then I learned to ride a bike. Follow me.

PREFACE

I'm writing this book because it's a shame that no one else already has. I aim to fix that. I first hesitated because I have read many great investment books and wondered what more I could add. Still, my financial, academic, and personal experiences ultimately convinced me that I indeed had a view worth expressing.

I was 33 when my father passed away. For the first time in my life, I instantly became responsible for something but lacked the essential prerequisite training. I was now the trustee of dad's trust; and mom was its sole beneficiary. This elephant in the room changed my life for good. How would my widowed mom now live happily without exhausting her retirement inheritance?

My dad was a faithful provider, but I had to institute a plan without him. So, with little experience or clear direction, I began a personal financial crusade armed only with my education, determination, and moral support from mom. I read about investments. I met brokers with mom and asked questions. I took seminars and did homework. My thirst for knowledge was insatiable. My only objective was to learn. Then one day, I witnessed other weekend students struggle and recognized that they might share the same challenge as my mom. Soon I was teaching, even though I originally had absolutely no such intention. This led me to discover the miracle of being taught by the subject myself when I thought I was just teaching it to others. I was still an eager student, and my teachers appeared on cue, sometimes unexpectedly out of thin air.

Although I had learned a fundamental approach to investing before the dot-com bubble peaked, it seemed that whatever advantage this gave me was soon lost when on-line trading arrived for good. In retrospect, maybe we were all spoiled by ten straight years of irrationally exuberant market returns, but in any case, it became clear that success demanded more than just being right. It meant being right on time or at least not at the wrong time. Just identifying a suitable investment was no longer good enough; when to buy or sell that investment was imperative as well.

I went for years before appreciating the merits of technical analysis. The idea that future investment prices could actually be forecasted by past prices initially made as much sense to me as driving my car to work while looking backward in my rear-view mirror to see where I had been instead of looking forward through my windshield to see where I was going. However, once it dawned on me that I really had nothing to lose, I found that even if charts and indicators were far from foolproof, they could often boost the odds of being right and reduce the risk of being wrong. So, choosing either fundamental or technical analysis and excluding the other was pointless because rational analysis combines the best of both approaches – to find the *RIGHT* asset and avoid the *WRONG* action at any particular time.

Building and managing your investment portfolio does not require rocket science or quantum physics. If you drive a car and buy your own groceries each week, you can learn to invest successfully. You need not trade often. In fact, investing is less stressful and time consuming when you don't rush. Consistency, discipline, and focus ultimately lead to prosperity. No one else will care about your lifelong financial success more than you will.

Although the future is inherently unpredictable, investing should never be haphazard. Many concepts commonly used to manage risk and reward in life also apply to investing. My investment approach has continued to evolve from humble beginnings over 25 years ago. I welcome you to read lessons I have learned along the way that I wish I knew much sooner. Without a guide, the long road to financial independence can seem like a maze. But you can win that marathon *INVESTING ON YOUR OWN TWO WHEELS.*

CONTENTS

CHAPTER 1

1) MOTIVATION: Let Your Money Work for You

Money isn't everything, but life with no money is difficult, if not impossible. I sometimes hear people say with despair that if they could merely hit the lottery, they would retire tomorrow. But since they know the chance of this outcome is tiny, they seem resigned to give up hope. Ambitions remain nothing more than dreams until you understand how to achieve them. Financial independence and freedom can be yours if you start with this end in mind. ***You can build your own fortune bit by bit instead of just wishing on a star.***

Suppose you saved $100 and earned a 1% investment return by the end of one month. Congratulations, you would now have $101. Instead of spending it all to celebrate, you repeat the process. In another month, your $101 becomes $102.01 and you also invest another $100 that grows to $101. Your running total now becomes $203.01. Repeat the process for a third month and you will have $205.04 plus $101 or $306.04. In 6 months, your total reaches $621.35. In 12 months, i.e., 1 year, you have $1,280.93. Future totals are: after 2 years = $2,724, 5 years = $8,249, 10 years = $23,234, 20 years = $99,915. Finally, after about 38 years you have $1,001,753. You added $100 faithfully to your investment portfolio for 463 consecutive months. Your $46,300 of total contributions snowballed by 12% per year into a million-dollar jackpot. Time is money.

You could be more or less fortunate. You might save more or less. Your investments might perform better or worse. Maybe 38 years is too long for you to wait. You can choose your own faster or slower path. The table below shows many ways to accumulate $1,000,000 by saving and investing. Circled figures match the case above. Tabulated values shaded green indicate less time required and those in red signal more time required.

Years to accumulate $1,000,000

Monthly Savings Rate

Compounded Annual Investment Return	$20	$50	$100	$200	$500	$1,000	$2,000
0%	Too long	Too long	Too long	Too long	Too long	Too long	41.7
1%	Too long	Too long	Too long	Too long	Too long	Too long	34.8
2%	Too long	Too long	Too long	Too long	Too long	49.1	30.3
3%	Too long	Too long	Too long	Too long	Too long	41.8	27.1
4%	Too long	Too long	Too long	Too long	Too long	36.7	24.6
5%	Too long	Too long	Too long	Too long	44.8	32.9	22.6
6%	Too long	Too long	Too long	Too long	40.1	29.9	20.9
7%	Too long	Too long	Too long	48.8	36.4	27.5	19.6
8%	Too long	Too long	Too long	44.3	33.4	25.5	18.4
9%	Too long	Too long	48.3	40.7	30.9	23.9	17.4
10%	Too long	Too long	44.5	37.7	28.8	22.4	16.5
11%	Too long	47.6	41.4	35.1	27.0	21.2	15.7
12%	Too long	44.4	38.7	32.9	25.5	20.1	15.0
13%	48.7	41.6	36.3	31.0	24.1	19.1	14.4
14%	45.8	39.2	34.3	29.3	22.9	18.2	13.8
15%	43.2	37.1	32.4	27.8	21.9	17.5	13.3
16%	40.9	35.2	30.8	26.5	20.9	16.8	12.8
17%	38.9	33.5	29.4	25.3	20.0	16.1	12.4
18%	37.1	31.9	28.1	24.2	19.2	15.5	12.0
19%	35.4	30.6	26.9	23.3	18.5	15.0	11.6
20%	33.9	29.3	25.8	22.4	17.8	14.5	11.3
21%	32.5	28.2	24.8	21.5	17.2	14.0	10.9
22%	31.3	27.1	23.9	20.8	16.6	13.6	10.6
23%	30.1	26.1	23.1	20.1	16.1	13.2	10.4
24%	29.1	25.2	22.3	19.4	15.6	12.8	10.1
25%	28.1	24.4	21.6	18.8	15.2	12.5	9.8

The time required to reach $1,000,000 depends on two key factors: how much you save each month and your compounded annual investment return. For example, if you can save $2,000 per month and invest those savings to earn 25% per year, you will reach the million-dollar milestone within 10 years. You could save $2,000 per month and still hit a million even if your investments earned 0% per year, but that would take much longer, 42 years. However, if you saved just $20 per month and your investments returned 15% each year, you would still achieve your goal in 43 years. Any saving rate and investment return combination which requires more than 45 working years is probably too long. After all, a 22 year-old college graduate would theoretically retire at 67, the standard age to collect Social Security benefits.

The graph below shows the same numbers with time plotted on the y-axis, the investment return on the x-axis, and a different color curve for each monthly savings rate. The previous table and the graph both tell the same story. *A continuous series of modest investments compounded over time will produce an astonishing sum that is within reach of nearly all working people before they retire.* You only need to live long enough to get rich. So, don't just dream of a winning lottery ticket. Create your own retirement fund instead. It will take you 10 to 45 years. The sooner you start, the more time you have, and the lower your savings rate needs to be. You can increase your likelihood of success, i.e., your margin of safety, by using a higher savings rate.

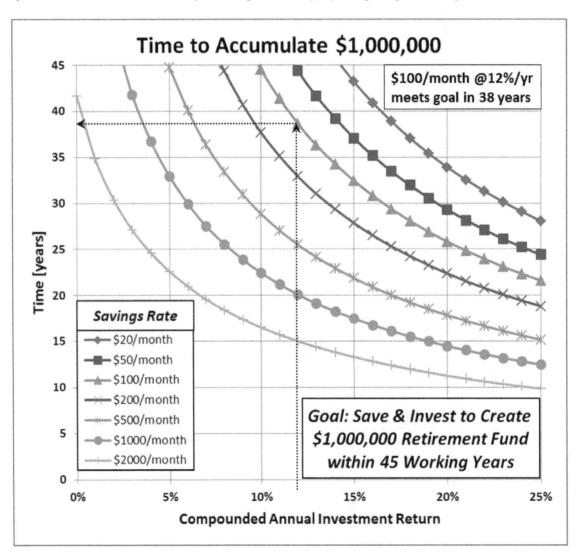

The goal upon retirement is not only that monthly savings will no longer be required, but furthermore that expenses will be covered for the rest of your life. So when you retire from work, your financial focus will shift from accumulating money to spending it. How long it will last also depends on two key factors: how much you spend each month and your compounded annual investment return. The table below shows many ways to disburse the million dollars accumulated. Values shaded green indicate longer times and those in red signal shorter times. Circled figures match the second example explained below.

$1 MM Monthly Investment Earnings			Years to spend $1,000,000						
			Monthly Spending Rate						
			$5,000	$5,800	$6,600	$7,300	$8,000	$8,700	$9,500
$0		0%	16.7	14.4	12.6	11.4	10.4	9.6	8.8
$833		1%	18.2	15.5	13.5	12.1	11.0	10.1	9.2
$1,667		2%	20.3	17.0	14.6	13.0	11.7	10.6	9.7
$2,500		3%	23.1	18.8	15.9	14.0	12.5	11.3	10.2
$3,333	Compounded Annual Investment Return	4%	27.5	21.4	17.6	15.3	13.5	12.1	10.8
$4,167		5%	35.9	25.4	20.0	17.0	14.7	13.1	11.6
$5,000		6%	Forever	33.1	23.7	19.3	16.4	14.3	12.5
$5,833		7%	Forever	Forever	30.8	23.0	18.7	15.9	13.6
$6,667		8%	Forever	Forever	Forever	30.7	22.5	18.2	15.2
$7,500		9%	Forever	Forever	Forever	Forever	30.9	22.1	17.4
$8,333		10%	Forever	Forever	Forever	Forever	Forever	31.8	21.1
$9,167		11%	Forever	Forever	Forever	Forever	Forever	Forever	30.6
$10,000		12%	Forever	Forever	Forever	Forever	Forever	Forever	Forever

Your $1,000,000 retirement fund will be exhausted within 9 years if you spend $9,500 per month and your investments earn 0% per year. However, if you spend $9,500 per month, your $1,000,000 will last forever if your investments earn 12% per year because those earnings amount to $10,000 per month. This example illustrates a simple but crucial financial commandment: ***EARN MORE THAN YOU SPEND***. The $1 million portfolio monthly investment earnings depend on the annual investment return. The specific dollar amount for each earnings rate is shown in the far left column. If you want your retirement fund to last forever, balance your spending to match your investment earnings. To best manage this, use a personal finance tool like Quicken.

Any spending rate and investment return combination which does not cover at least 30 retirement years is probably not good enough. After all, a 67 year-old retiree would theoretically have a life expectancy of 87. It would be smart to be covered for 10 years longer. Plan to have your money to outlive you even though you can't take it with you once you are gone.

The 0% to 12% annual investment return range listed in the spending table reflects more conservative investments for an older investor with more wealth at risk and a shorter time horizon for growth. The 0% to 25% investment return range shown before in the accumulation table implies more aggressive investments suitable for a younger investor with less wealth to lose and a longer time horizon to realize growth.

The graph on the next page shows the spending table numbers with time plotted on the y-axis, the investment return on the x-axis, and a different color curve for each spending rate. The table and matching graph again tell the same story. ***The investment fund created during your working career will cover retirement expenses for life when properly invested.*** Your personal retirement fund will work so one day you won't have to.

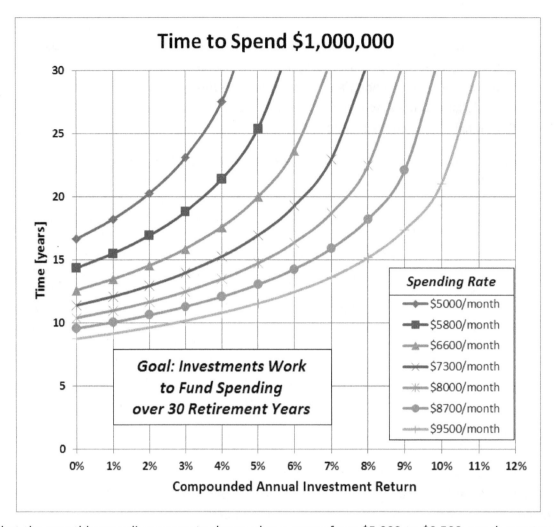

Notice that the monthly spending amounts shown above range from $5,000 to $9,500, much greater than the monthly contributions that ranged from $20 to $2,000. This fact makes sense for two reasons. First, most people find it impossible to save more than they spend during their working years. Even if you can save and invest 25% of your gross income, the other 75% that you spend is 3 times more. If you save 10% of your income, the other 90% that you spend is 9 times more. Second, inflation guarantees that your future expenses will be higher for the same lifestyle that you enjoy today. For example, expenses will cost 2 times more in 30 years assuming that inflation averages 2.45% per year; and at this rate, expenses will run 3 times more in 45 years. ***Anticipate that future retirement spending will be roughly 25 times your original savings rate.*** Save and invest as much as possible as soon as you can to help offset this inequity. Learn to live on just 75% of earnings each year, and make trouble with money disappear.

Although a $1 million retirement fund was used to illustrate the mathematics of compounding, your goals might be different. For example, you might decide to save twice as much while you still work and then spend twice as much during retirement. In that case, the times to reach $2 million and then spend it would be identical to those already listed. However, if your savings rate, retirement fund goal, and spending rate combination is not a simple multiple of the original example, the figures will change even though the principles are the same. See Appendix A for discrete compound interest formulas to calculate your own figures using the compound amount factor for saving and the capital recovery factor for spending. Riggs [ref 1] provides further details.

CHAPTER 2

2) __BEHAVIORAL ECONOMICS: Understanding Investment Decisions__

Once your path to reach financial independence is clear, you may be eager to start. However, this goal will test your will power against your impulses. *Consider the following quandary for reference:* Would you rather have one marshmallow now or two later - a bird in the hand or two in the bush?

In 1960, psychologist Walter Mischel first offered this proposal to four-year old boys and girls attending Bing Nursery School at Stanford University. His original incentive was to understand how his own impulsive young daughters learned to exercise self-control. While some children devoured the single marshmallow soon after the proctor left the room to "complete an errand", other children were able to resist temptation for 15 minutes until the proctor returned to fulfill the two-marshmallow reward. These children displayed a variety of behaviors to delay gratification such as covering their eyes, turning around to look away, kicking the desk, tugging their hair, or even caressing the marshmallow like a stuffed animal.

More revealing results came after the first follow up study in 1988. Teenagers who had waited for the two marshmallows as preschoolers were more likely to score higher on the Scholastic Aptitude Test. They were also more likely to be rated by their parents as having a greater ability to plan, handle stress, respond to reason, exhibit self-control in frustrating situations, and concentrate without becoming distracted.

True intelligence is smart thought followed by commensurate action. According to Daniel Goleman [ref 2], our emotional aptitude determines how well we can use our innate mental abilities and other skills to succeed. Emotional intelligence includes self-motivation, persistence despite frustration, impulse control, gratification delay, mood regulation, and thinking amidst distress. Your ability to manage your emotions in general and delayed gratification in particular may ultimately determine your long-term investment success more than any other single factor.

2.1 __Psychological Warfare: Beware of Your Own Behavior__

Quantitative analysis of investor behavior since 1994 has shown that the average investor consistently earns less than stock market benchmarks [Dalbar, ref 3]. Psychological traps, triggers, and misconceptions induce normal investors to act irrationally and make systematic errors. Biased behaviors that lead to poor decision-making include over-optimism, overconfidence, regret, loss aversion, herding, media response, and cognitive errors in perception, judgment, and reasoning. Such behavior leads to buying and selling at the wrong time and, more importantly, reduced long-term success by not holding investments for more than a few years. Establishing logical and methodical decision-making processes can help investors avoid these errors. ***"Investing is most intelligent when it is most businesslike."*** Those are, says legendary investor Warren Buffett, "the nine most important words ever written about investing."

You will have to wait before you reap investment rewards. Although controlling your emotions is easy when everything goes right, you will get distracted, frustrated, and stressed when everything does not go your way. Many things can go wrong. Wage and price controls, oil embargoes, business scandals, nuclear accidents, political crises, terrorist attacks, financial failures, environmental catastrophes, pandemic diseases, and wars have all occurred within the past fifty years. Personal obligations will also claim time, energy, and attention you could otherwise devote to your finances. Before you know it, you may feel like you are losing control.

The best way to handle a risky situation is to mitigate or avoid it completely by planning ahead. Notice your own attitude and response to both success and failure. Tailor your investments and strategies in advance to match your temperament. Anticipate the cases where you may need to be saved from yourself. Build some protection against your own tendencies into your overall behavior. Your sense of control comes from your ability to choose how you will respond to any outcome.

The investment results you experience shape your behavior over time. Every decision and transaction you make or skip affects your psychological perspective. This reality is actually a key component of your training. As shown below, emotions are triggered by just four possible outcomes depending on whether or not you own an investment and whether its price goes up or down over a particular time frame.

INVESTMENT OUTCOMES

		PRICE WENT UP	PRICE WENT DOWN
YOU OWN IT (Participant)		You have a gain	You have a loss
YOU DON'T OWN IT (Bystander)		You missed a gain	You missed a loss

1) YOU OWN IT - You have a gain: Happy you already bought and/or relieved you did not yet sell
   "To those who use well what they are given, even more will be given, and they will have abundance."
   - Matthew 25:29

2) YOU OWN IT - You have a loss: Sad you already bought and/or upset you did not yet sell
   "A fool and his money are soon parted." - John Bridges

3) YOU DON'T OWN IT - You missed a loss: Happy you already sold and/or relieved you did not yet buy
   "A penny saved is a penny earned."

4) YOU DON'T OWN IT - You missed a gain: Sad you already sold and/or upset you did not yet buy
   "Nothing ventured, nothing gained."

Warning! The stakes here are a quantum leap higher than the marshmallow quandary. The worst outcome in Mishel's proposal was still rewarding. Getting just a single marshmallow now is no skin off of your nose. Investing generates additional emotional pressure because you risk assets that you already have. A loss leaves you worse off than not investing at all. However, you can completely eliminate this risk simply by holding cash instead of holding investments. The fear of losing what he already has would drive a four-year old boy to sleep with his coin cache safely under his pillow each night. But Mishel's students never even had to consider potential losses as a punishment. Investing thus transcends nursery school.

Around 1930, Harvard psychologist B.F. Skinner studied behavior conditioning by training lab animals to perform specific actions in response to a stimulus such as sound or light. He created a chamber, now known as a Skinner box, which delivered a reward (e.g. food) to reinforce correctly performed behavior as well as punishment (e.g. electric shock) for incorrect or missing responses. The test subjects eventually learned by trial and error how to interpret signals and then operate a lever to collect the prize and avoid the penalty. They became trained by the carrot and the stick.

Skinner Operant Conditioning Chamber

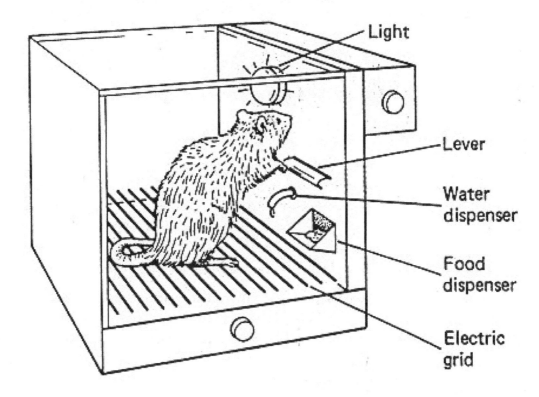

This same punishment or reward dichotomy can make investing feel like an operant conditioning chamber that provokes fear and greed. However, under the right circumstances, you might willingly consent to being the subject animal in the Skinner box. Specifically, if the punishment was tolerable, the reward was truly gratifying, and you got rewarded way more often than punished, the whole experience would be attractive instead of repulsive. But if the penalty was too severe, the prize was marginal, or the penalty came more frequently than the prize, you might prefer to skip the whole experiment and just watch it yourself instead.

Consider every investment as a compromise between how well you want to eat versus how well you want to sleep, i.e., greed versus fear. Fear means distress aroused by an impending threat. Greed is excessive desire for wealth. Investing can foster greed to make money and greed to give none back. Investing can also breed fear of losing money and Fear of Missing Out (FOMO). Every buyer wants to capitalize on a golden opportunity to get in near ground floor before the price rises, but also avoid being cut by a falling knife when the price drops. Therefore, buy before the price goes up, but don't buy before the price goes down. Every seller wants to lock in profits or at least break even before the price drops, but also avoid leaving money on the table when the price rises. So, sell before the price goes down, but don't sell before the price goes up. Simple, except for one detail: nobody ever knows for sure which way, how far, or how fast the price will move next.

Hindsight has perfect vision, but foresight is flawed. The yin and yang inherent in buying and selling trigger delight, remorse, relief, anxiety, paralysis, and more. If you merely react to them, you can become a slave to these emotions. But you can master them if you are proactive and take charge instead. You need a strategy to combat this psychological warfare. Successful investing requires an operating system just like a computer.

Steve Jobs envisioned a world where every human effectively used a computer. To him it was the most remarkable tool ever invented, like a bicycle for the mind. A bicycle converts human metabolic energy into forward motion remarkably well. In 1973, Oxford University engineer S.S. Wilson reported that a human riding a bicycle moves three to four times faster and uses five times less energy compared to walking [Wilson, ref 4]. This boost in performance makes the cyclist much more efficient than a jet, a horse, a salmon or any other locomotion machine or animal. Your investment system makes the difference between consistently productive results and pedestrian performance instead. It is your bike to ride en route to your retirement fund destination.

2.2 Quantitative Relief: Game and Decision Theory, Probability, & Expected Value

A game is a contest whose action is governed by rules and result is determined by skill, strength, or chance. Used as a verb, game means to compete for a stake. Chess is a game of skill. The outcome is not based on luck. Only the series of decisions made by each chess player determines who wins or loses. Bingo is a game of chance. The result does not involve skill. Instead, a randomizing device such as dice, playing cards, or numbered balls dictates the outcome. Backgammon and other games involve elements of both chance and skill. *Skill is exercised whenever you make a decision and act. Chance takes over whenever you don't.*

Suppose you received $1 for a correct coin flip prediction but were obligated to pay $1 instead for an incorrect prediction. Although you might enjoy the thrill of calling heads or tails, after several rounds you would probably soon realize that your chance of winning was the same as your chance of losing. Indeed, a coin toss is a simple and unbiased way used to decide an arbitrary alternative. Thus, you eventually might conclude this game was a waste of your time because you only break even.

But, you could play a different game. Suppose you received $5 for a correct prediction when a single cube of dice was rolled but were obligated to pay $1 instead for an incorrect prediction. Your payoff looks more enticing and your penalty is no worse. However, your chance of winning is now just 1/5 your chance of losing because the dice cube has 5 other sides not showing when 1 side is face up. It turns out that this game is also no better than the coin flip in the long run.

Winning games that are better than break even do exist. The challenge is to recognize them and take appropriate action. For example, if you received $5 for a correct coin flip prediction and paid only $1 for a wrong one, you would soon find that game profitable. In contrast, if you only received $1 for a correct dice roll guess and still paid $1 for a wrong one, you would ultimately lose money. The expected value of a gamble quantifies its ultimate worth based on the payoffs and probabilities of all possible outcomes. To calculate the expected value of an uncertain wager, first multiply the payoff of each outcome by the chance that it will occur, and then add up the results for all possible outcomes.

For example, the expected value of the first coin flip example is $0

Expected value = Payoff 1 x Probability 1 + Payoff 2 x Probability 2

Expected value = $1 x (1/2) + (-$1) x (1/2) = $0.50 - $0.50 = $0

Likewise, the expected value of the second coin flip example is $2

Expected value = Payoff 1 x Probability 1 + Payoff 2 x Probability 2

Expected value = $5 x (1/2) + (-$1) x (1/2) = $2.50 - $0.50 = $2

The expected value of the first dice roll example is $0

Expected value = Payoff 1 x Probability 1 + Payoff 2 x Probability 2 + … + Payoff 6 x Probability 6

Expected value = $5 x (1/6) - $1 x (1/6) - $1 x (1/6) - $1 x (1/6) - $1 x (1/6) - $1 x (1/6)

Expected value = $0.833 – $0.167 – $0.167 – $0.167 – $0.167 – $0.167 = $0

Finally, the expected value of the second dice roll example is -$0.667

Expected value = Payoff 1 x Probability 1 + Payoff 2 x Probability 2 + … + Payoff 6 x Probability 6

Expected value = $1 x (1/6) - $1 x (1/6) - $1 x (1/6) - $1 x (1/6) - $1 x (1/6) - $1 x (1/6)

Expected value = $1 x (1/6) - $1 x (5/6) = $0.167 - $0.833 = -$0.667

In gambling, the odds are the ratio of the payoff to the wager. If a bet is fair, then the odds offered perfectly match the outcome probabilities. A fair bet that a die will roll a six pays the gambler $5 and returns the original $1 wager when a six occurs, but forfeits the $1 wager in every other case. The bet terms are fair, because on average, for every roll that gives a six and a net $5 payout, five other rolls don't produce a six and together cost $5. Since the gains offset the losses exactly, gambling ultimately yields no benefit here. However, if the odds don't match the statistical probabilities, then one betting party has an advantage over the other. For instance, casinos guarantee their profits to stay in business by setting the odds in their own favor.

Although I have visited Las Vegas several times, my casino losses total less than $20. Expected value is the reason why. A bet is only favorable when its expected value is positive. ***So, the difference between investing and gambling boils down to a minus sign.*** If you place a $1 bet on RED in American Roulette, your chances of winning are 18/38 because 18 of 38 numbers are red, 18 are black, and 2 are green. The payoff if you win is $1, the same amount you bet. The expected value of this wager is a 5.26 cent loss.

Expected value = $1 x (18/38) - $1 x (20/38) = - $0.0526

Your expected loss is the casino's inherent advantage designed to capture your original $1 within about 19 bets. Although gambling can be entertainment, it is not profitable investing. Since I don't play to lose, games like this I watch instead. Other casino games invariably have an expected value worse than roulette.

A $1 lottery ticket can win millions, but most people never consider the jackpot chances before they play. Suppose a $1 million jackpot is awarded for a ticket that matches all 6 numbers drawn from a field of 49. Since the order of the numbers drawn does not matter, the probability they all match is given by the combinations of 49 items taken 6 at a time, that is, 1 in 13,983,816. So, the expected value of Lotto is

Expected value = ($1,000,000 - $1) x (1/13,983,816) - $1 x (13,983,815/13,983,816) = - $0.928

In other words, this lottery gets to keep 92.8% of ticket revenues and only pays out 7.2% for jackpots. By comparison, the lottery almost makes roulette look good. Paying $1 per ticket to hit a $1,000,000 jackpot is clearly a losing proposal since it takes nearly 14,000,000 tries to successfully match 6 numbers. (But if you save $1 per ticket and invest it at 12% instead 46,300 times over 38 years, a $1,000,000 jackpot is yours.)

Just knowing the expected value is a first step towards more sensible wagers. In poker, pot odds are used to determine the expected value of a hand that could win the pot if a future card is drawn. Pot odds are the ratio between the cost to bet and the pot's current size. The player poised to bet compares the pot odds to the chance of drawing a winning card. When the probability of a winning card exceeds the pot odds, the expected value is positive. You stand to win more money on average than it costs to call the bet. When the chances of a winning card are less than the pot odds, the expected value is negative. You win less money on average than it costs to call the bet. The expected value for the 6 number lottery example is negative since the winning chances are just 1/13,983,816 and the pot odds are $1/$1,000,000. ***Never make bets you can't expect to win.***

The next step to capitalize on more winning situations is to improve the expected value by increasing the payoff relative to the risk and/or raising the payoff probability. For example, counting cards in blackjack can swing the probability a few percent to give the player an advantage instead of originally favoring the house. Since each deck dealt out includes four suits of thirteen cards, keeping a running count of the cards already seen enables a player to infer which cards must be remaining in the deck. The player then bets more when the chances are good and less when they aren't. Even though unaided card counting is legal in the U.S., this approach proved to be so effective that casinos responded with aggressive tactics to relentlessly detect and thwart it. Nevertheless, courts have ruled that this use of intelligent strategy is not cheating.

A less hostile example of expected value in action now routinely occurs in every basketball game. An NBA player scores points for his team each time the ball goes through the basket when he shoots. A shot from within 23 feet scores two points; a shot from outside 23 feet scores three points. Teams are not penalized for any shots they miss. The best way any basketball player can improve the probability of making a shot is simply to launch it closer to the basket. Statistics confirm this observation. In the 2017-18 season, NBA players made 46.0% of all shots taken. [Basketball-Reference, ref 5] This figure includes 36.2% for 3-point shots and 51.0% for 2-point shots. Based on these chances alone, you might think the winning strategy would always be to shoot as many two-pointers as possible. However, it depends on the expected values for both shot types.

Expected values for NBA shots 2017-2018

3-pointers: $3 \times (0.362) = 1.086$ 2-pointers: $2 \times (0.510) = 1.020$

Expected values for NBA shots 1979-1980

3-pointers: $3 \times (0.280) = 0.840$ 2-pointers: $2 \times (0.487) = 0.975$

The 3-point shot has forever changed the way basketball is played. When first introduced in the 1979-80 season, NBA teams attempted less than 3 of these shots per game, typically when time expired at the end of a quarter. Just 28.0% of 3-pointers were good that year. But, in 2017-18, NBA teams attempted 29 3-pointers per game and 36.2% were good. The ratio of 3-point shot attempts to 2-point shot attempts per game was 29 to 57 in 2017-18, but it was only 3 to 87 back in 1979-80. Thus, within 38 years, the 3-pointer has gone from a last second gimmick shot to an essential scoring strategy mainly because it now has a greater expected value than the conventional 2-point shot does [Mather, ref 6].

All these examples illustrate how valuable probability and statistics can be when the results are uncertain. Positive expected value ventures are essential to every successful investment system. The expected value is crucial because it quantifies the Skinner box proposed by any investment. ***In fact, expected value can be applied to design investment opportunities defined by tolerable risk, satisfying reward, and favorable chances.*** Price zones establish the potential risk versus reward, i.e., the pot odds. Technical indicators can help signal when circumstances favor sellers or buyers more than the other, i.e., the probability of loss or gain. For best success, set your expectations in advance so you are ready to capitalize whenever opportunity knocks.

CHAPTER 3

3) <u>TIME HORIZONS & INVESTMENT RISK</u>: When You Need Money, No Cash Means Danger

To pick the right investments, you must first know how soon you will need your money back. That future date is the investment time horizon. If you need to liquidate an investment instantly, the time horizon would be just a second. If an investment need not be sold until you die, the time horizon would be the rest of your life. Your best investment always depends on how long you can wait for its return. ***To maximize your chance of success, match each investment to its time horizon.***

A financial goal ultimately lies behind every investment and declares the reason why you choose to save money instead of spending it now. A short-term investment goal has a time horizon within three years. A medium-term investment goal has a three to ten year time horizon. A long-term investment goal has a horizon beyond ten years. Although you can accrue enough money for a new car down payment in the short term, you will need more time to accumulate the down payment on a house. And to amass enough wealth to retire from work indefinitely, you must implement a long-term strategy.

The figure below compares the historical performance of stocks and bonds. Green figures show average (geometric mean) returns; vertical gray bars depict return ranges. Although bond returns have typically exceeded inflation, stock returns have generally been far superior [Schiller, FRED, Yahoo, ref 7-9]. But, a higher average annual investment return inevitably implies a higher variance. So the return for any specific period has a greater chance of actually landing further from the average than expected. Fluctuating returns create an investment dilemma, i.e., a sure bird in the hand versus maybe two in the bush instead.

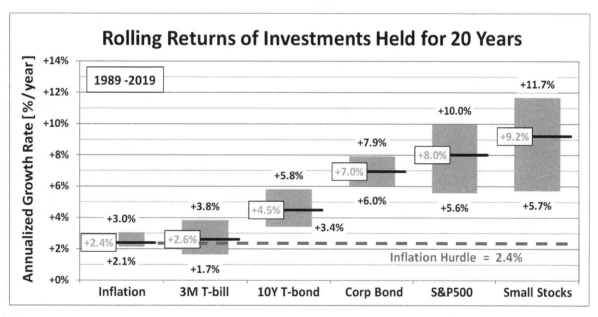

Most bonds are debts issued by corporations and federal, state, or local governments to borrow money used to finance projects and operations. Bonds are held by investors who periodically receive fixed interest payments until the bond matures and the original principal lent is completely repaid. Bonds are fixed income loans characterized by the debt duration and credit rating, i.e., the worthiness of the issuer to repay the debt. The US Treasury issues bonds that mature in 30 years or less (T-bonds). Money market instruments are fixed income contracts that mature within 12 months, e.g., US Treasury bills (T-bills) and certificates of deposit (CDs). Money market funds represent short-term savings accounts intended to not lose money and hopefully beat inflation.

Stocks entitle the owner to shares of a corporation's earnings and assets, i.e., equity. Bondholders have no such claim. Some corporations pay stock dividends comparable to bond interest, but stock returns are not limited to dividends alone. Capital appreciation can also potentially provide a much greater reward. But, if a company fails, creditors and bond holders are paid in full before stockholders receive any money. Unlike bond owners, stockholders never have any assurance of recovering their original investment. Thus, stocks are riskier, but can often be more rewarding than bonds when the corporate earnings grow significantly.

A trailing return compares the current value of an investment to its value at a previous time such as a day, a week, a month, or a year earlier. A rolling return is a series of trailing returns that extend back in time to capture the history of how this comparison has changed. A trailing return is a single snapshot; a rolling return includes many snapshots that animate the true investment story. Rolling returns should ideally express how investment gains are spread around their average. This demonstrates performance and consistency during both good and bad times. The figure below shows that short-term rolling returns for stocks averaged about 10% since 1989. However, the range of short-term stock returns was alarming. Although the best returns were big gains, the worst returns were huge losses.

Best, Worst, and Average Short-term Investment Returns (1 & 2 Years)

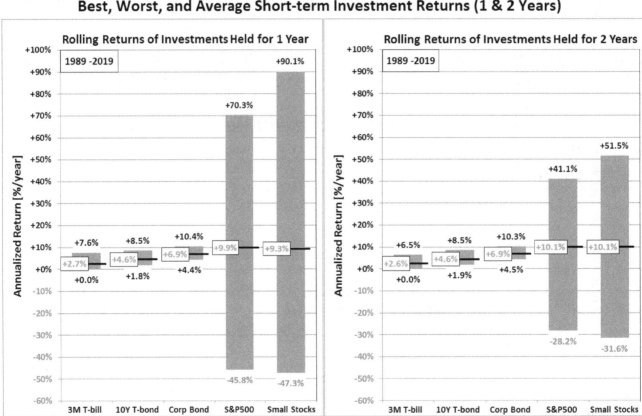

For the Standard & Poor's 500 stock index (S&P 500), 79% of one-year trailing returns beat inflation. However, over 17% of one-year trailing returns were losses; the worst one was -46% between March 2008 and March 2009. For small-company stocks, 71% of one-year trailing returns beat inflation. But, over 24% of one-year trailing returns were losses; the worst one was -47% between March 2008 and March 2009. It would take nearly seven years to recover from such large losses if the +10% average growth then resumed.

Results for two-year trailing returns were similar, but more tempered. For the S&P 500 index, 82% of two-year trailing returns beat inflation. However, 17% of two-year trailing returns were losses; the worst one was -28% between March 2007 and March 2009. For small-company stocks, 80% of two-year trailing returns beat inflation. But, over 15% of two-year trailing returns were losses; the worst one was -32% between March 2007 and March 2009. It would take about four years to recover from these losses if the +10% average growth then resumed.

Risky assets can generate large losses as shown in red. Conservative assets offer little reward beyond inflation. Although over 70% of short-term stock returns beat inflation, the risk of large losses still made stocks unfit for short time horizons. ***Money market funds are the much safer short-term investment alternative to stocks.***

The figure below shows that the risk versus reward performance of stocks was better over a medium-term time horizon. The average rolling return was still 10%, but the risk of the worst loss was clearly less than the reward of the best gain.

Best, Worst, and Average Medium-term Investment Returns (3 & 5 Years)

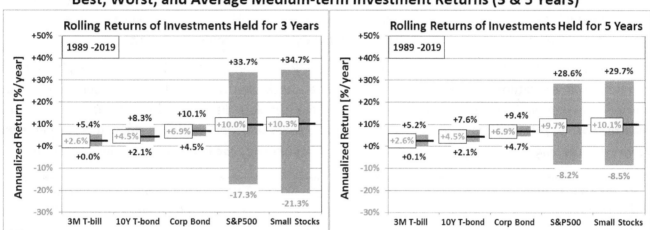

For the S&P 500 stock index, 79% of three-year trailing returns beat inflation. About 18% of three-year trailing returns were losses; the worst one was -17% between March 2006 and March 2009. For small-company stocks, 87% of three-year trailing returns beat inflation. But, 9% of three-year trailing returns were losses; the worst one was -21% between March 2006 and March 2009. It would take over two years to recover from these losses if the +10% average growth then resumed.

Results for five-year trailing stock returns were even more palatable. For the S&P 500 index, 71% of five-year trailing returns beat inflation. Although 16% of five-year trailing returns were losses, the worst one was -8% between March 2004 and March 2009. For small-company stocks, 85% of five-year trailing returns beat inflation. But, only 6% of five-year trailing returns were losses; the worst one was -8% between March 2004 and March 2009. It would take just one year to recover from these losses if the +10% average growth then resumed.

The risk of smaller losses made stocks more tempting for medium time horizons. Although some investors might choose bonds in this situation to play it safe, other investors might prefer stocks despite the peril.

The figure on the next page shows that the risk versus reward performance of stocks was best over a long-term time horizon. The average rolling return was still 10%, but the risk of the worst loss was minimal.

Best, Worst, and Average Long-term Investment Returns (10 & 15 Years)

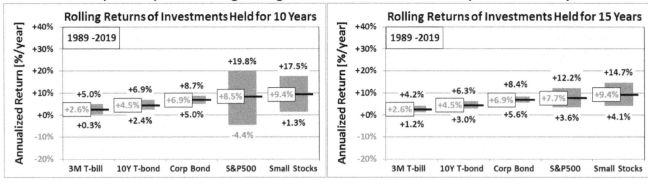

For the S&P 500 index, 88% of ten-year trailing returns beat inflation. About 9% of ten-year trailing returns were losses; the worst one was just -4% between March 1999 and March 2009. For small-company stocks, over 99% of ten-year trailing returns beat inflation. No ten-year trailing returns were losses; the worst return was +1.3%.

Results for fifteen-year trailing returns were all positive. For the S&P 500 index, 100% of fifteen-year trailing returns beat inflation. The worst fifteen-year trailing return was +3.6%. For small-company stocks, 100% of fifteen-year trailing returns beat inflation. The worst fifteen-year trailing return was +4.1%.

Stocks were the right choice for long time horizons because losses were small and infrequent. Long-term fixed income investment returns were much less rewarding than stock returns. The tables below summarize stock rolling returns for all time horizons; see Appendix B for the complete distribution of S&P 500 rolling returns. ***Over the past 30 years and more, the prescription to avoid losses and make money in stocks was to hold them as investments long enough to overcome short-term fluctuations and reap long-term compounded returns.***

Risk vs. Time Horizon: Large Stocks (S&P 500)					Risk vs. Time Horizon: Small Stocks (S&P600)			
	Years	% Losses	Worst Return	>INFLATION		Years	% Losses	Worst Return	>INFLATION
Short-term	1	17%	-45.8%	79%	Short-term	1	24%	-47.3%	71%
	2	17%	-28.2%	82%		2	15%	-31.6%	80%
	3	18%	-17.3%	79%		3	9%	-21.3%	87%
	5	16%	-8.2%	71%		5	6%	-8.5%	85%
Long-term	10	9%	-4.4%	88%	Long-term	10	0%	1.3%	100%
	15	0%	3.6%	100%		15	0%	4.1%	100%
	20	0%	5.6%	100%		20	0%	5.7%	100%

Although these results are not certain to repeat in the future, they do suggest a successful strategy. ***Risky assets are not appropriate for short time horizons.*** An investor who must sell a variable asset at a loss to cover an expected commitment has made a big mistake. ***Conservative assets are not productive for long time horizons.*** An investor who never tolerates any unrealized short-term loss will severely stunt long-term growth. Over a lifetime of investing for retirement, the policy of being too cautious is the greatest risk of all.

Strive to fully understand your investment portfolio risk and your tolerance to withstand it *BEFORE* you invest your money! Risk is not a four-letter curse word once you recognize that it not only means a potential loss, but also the chance to make higher returns.

CHAPTER 4

4)   WHORT TO OWN: Know The Merchandise - Buy Growth

The size, number, or value of anything that develops or increases shows the same general trend over time. Whether it is a child's height or weight, a population count, or a bank account balance, growth means more now than before, and more later than now. Decay, the opposite of growth, means less now than before, and less later than now. Equilibrium is a perfect balance between equally opposed growth and decay.

A plot of any amount versus time that shows an incline or positive slope signals growth. A decline or negative slope signals decay. A level with no slope indicates equilibrium. The plots of growth, equilibrium, and decay designated below each give a simple picture to keep in mind whenever a potential investment candidate is considered. The verdict always answers one single question: ***Will this investment's future value be significantly higher than its current value before the time horizon arrives?*** In other words, will time bring growth instead of dormancy or decay before the investment deadline is reached? Since money is invested to make profits, any ***investments that do not grow steadily are counterproductive to reaching your retirement fund goal on time.***

Universal Phases of Development

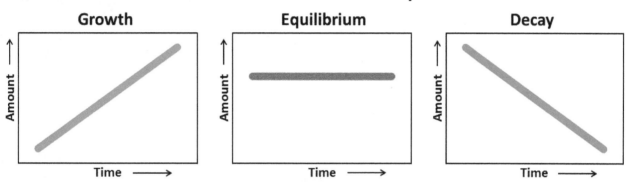

If you own an investment marked by growth, the playing field tilts in your favor. The trajectory is up. You can ride the current. Equilibrium has a flat trajectory. The playing field is neutral. You merely tread water if you own an investment like this. The trajectory of decay goes down. The playing field tilts against you. You swim against the current if your investment does this. However, growth, equilibrium, and decay are rarely mutually exclusive; they are typically interspersed over time instead. For instance, a growth spurt might be followed by a stagnant pause before a long decay. Or, an abrupt decline may soon stabilize and begin a gradual recovery. Decay may stair-step down and growth may stair-step up. There is a season to everything.

The Standard and Poor's 500 index tracks the 500 largest publically traded U.S. companies and covers 80% of the total domestic stock market value. The progress of the S&P 500 from 1990 to 2020 is shown (on a logarithmic scale) in the first figure on the next page. Annual growth (total return including reinvested dividends) averaged 10% over 31 years, but wide variations were common. Periods of faster growth as well as drastic downturns are reflected by the 19% annual standard deviation.

A severe, sharp drop that reverses a long steady climb is unnerving. No other stock chart pattern warrants more vigilant attention. However, after straying too far in either direction from its long-term average trajectory, the price then got back on track despite temporary deviations off course. This compensating tendency to maintain a stable, lasting trend is known as "mean reversion" and has been characteristic of US stocks for many decades.

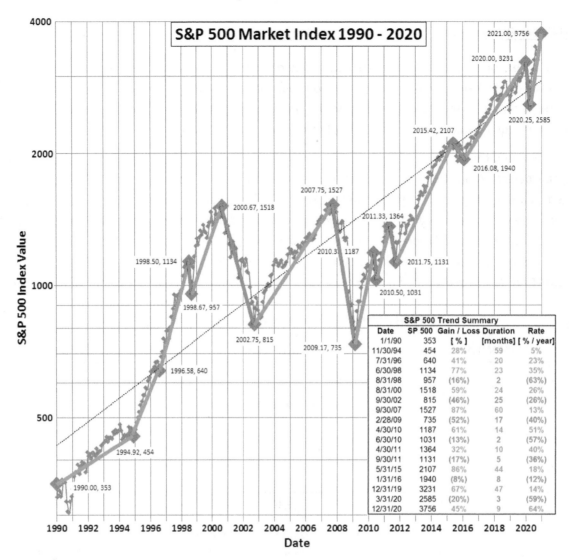

S&P 500 Trend Summary				
Date	SP 500	Gain / Loss [%]	Duration [months]	Rate [% / year]
1/1/90	353			
11/30/94	454	28%	59	5%
7/31/96	640	41%	20	23%
6/30/98	1134	77%	23	35%
8/31/98	957	(16%)	2	(63%)
8/31/00	1518	59%	24	26%
9/30/02	815	(46%)	25	(26%)
9/30/07	1527	87%	60	13%
2/28/09	735	(52%)	17	(40%)
4/30/10	1187	61%	14	51%
6/30/10	1031	(13%)	2	(57%)
4/30/11	1364	32%	10	40%
9/30/11	1131	(17%)	5	(36%)
5/31/15	2107	86%	44	18%
1/31/16	1940	(8%)	8	(12%)
12/31/19	3231	67%	47	14%
3/31/20	2585	(20%)	3	(59%)
12/31/20	3756	45%	9	64%

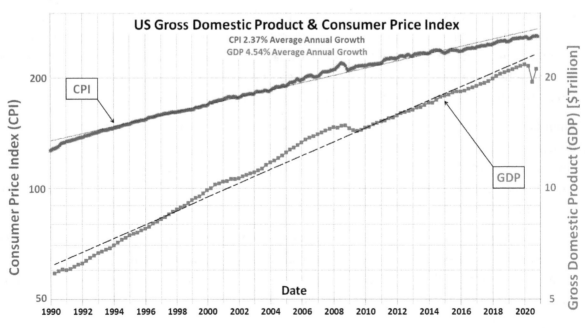

Despite its variability, the 10% average S&P 500 return was significantly higher than the 4.5% average U.S. Gross Domestic Product. GDP is the value of goods and services produced in a country, a comprehensive measure of its economic activity. The previous chart also shows that GDP was higher than the steady 2.4% average U.S. Consumer Price Index growth rate. The CPI, a gauge of inflation, measures the prices paid by urban consumers for most household goods and services. ***The CPI represents the absolute minimum growth threshold for any viable investment. The S&P 500 companies are logical investment candidates because they typically grow faster than inflation. In fact, they often grow faster than the overall economy as well.***

One successful (trillion-dollar) company included in the S&P 500 index is Alphabet. Its progress from 2004 to 2020 is shown in the figure below. The 24% average annual growth rate (price appreciation) with still tolerable variations over 16 years is exceptional. Even other well-known, blue-chip companies, like Boeing, Chevron, Johnson & Johnson, Verizon, and Walmart have not fared nearly as well. And these are a handful of the thirty well-established, financially sound companies that comprise the Dow Jones Industrial Average.

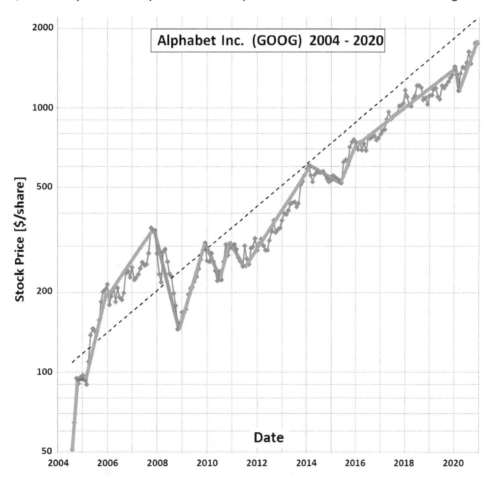

4.1 Stock Market Investments - Organization and Classification

Individual companies are like individual people; they generally grow fast when young, become stable in their prime, and ultimately may decline. The bigger they grow, the harder it becomes to grow bigger. A company can go bankrupt, split into separate parts, or merge with another company. All publicly traded companies are in business to make money. They report sales and earnings each quarter just like students get report cards to periodically document performance.

Key financial reports for companies are similar to those for individuals. The first kind tallies assets (credits) minus liabilities (debts) to determine an individual's net worth or a company's book value. This report is known as the balance sheet and states the present financial position. The second kind of financial report details revenues (money received) less costs (money spent) to determine net earnings over a time period such as a quarter-year or full year. This report is known as the income statement and indicates how the financial position is changing with time. Together, these two statements are essential for the same reason that a map and compass are used for navigation during any journey. To figure the time and distance to reach your destination, you must know where you start and the speed and direction you travel.

The U.S. Securities and Exchange Commission (SEC) requires public companies to file Form 10-K to summarize their annual financial performance. Form 10-K includes information for the year's final fiscal quarter as well. The three other fiscal quarters are reported on SEC Form 10-Q. Consolidated financial statements are also included at the end of the annual report published by each company for its shareholders. These documents all include important data, but the volume of information is often overwhelming for an individual investor to readily absorb. The Value Line Investment Survey provides stock reports of public companies including analysis, opinion, and Timeliness & Safety ranks - free online for all 30 Dow Jones Industrial Average stocks. ***No single page will tell you more about a stock than its Value Line report.*** (See Alphabet Inc. example, [ref 10])

Mutual funds and exchange-traded funds (ETF's) offer investors stocks (and/or bonds) grouped together for purchase or sale in a single package. The stocks held by most mutual funds are bought and sold by professional money managers. Stocks held by most ETF's are automatically traded to meet conditions stipulated by whatever objective or index the fund was designed to track. These funds may hold tens, hundreds, or even thousands of individual stocks (and/or bonds). Consequently, learning the true character of an investment fund can be a monumental task. Morningstar, Inc. publishes comprehensive summaries on investment funds including their Rating, Style, Holdings, and Performance. Morningstar classifies stock funds by average company size (small/mid/large cap) versus investment style (value/blend/growth). Bond funds are classified by debt quality versus duration (short/intermediate/long). ***No single source will tell you more about a mutual fund or ETF than its Morningstar report.*** (See the S&P 500 Fund example, [ref 11])

To uniquely identify its shares traded on a public stock exchange, every stock, ETF, and mutual fund has its own ticker symbol, an abbreviation used to place buy and sell orders. Stock and ETF ticker symbols contain four or fewer characters. Mutual fund tickers typically have five characters and end with an X. Ticker symbol characters are all upper case. The Alphabet Inc. ticker is GOOG. The Vanguard S&P 500 ETF ticker is VOO. Like stocks, ETFs trade during the day at their market price. Mutual funds trade at the day's closing price, the net asset value.

It is now easy to establish an investment account with a reputable brokerage firm such as Charles Schwab, TD Ameritrade, Fidelity, or E*TRADE. In many cases, stock and ETF trades are now commission-free, and minimum account balances are zero. Fractional stock shares or "slices" can be purchased today with as little as $1 as well.

Be sure to specify the correct account type because it governs how and when your money is taxed. A traditional 401(k) plan or individual retirement account (IRA) is completely tax-deferred because all contributions and investment earnings are not taxed until they are withdrawn. But, investment earnings and valid withdrawals from a Roth IRA or 401(k) plan are tax-free forever because all contributions are fully taxed before they are deposited. Finally, after-tax money is deposited into a taxable, non-retirement account, but investment interest, dividends, and realized capital gains are taxed in each year received. See Rodgers [ref 12] for more details.

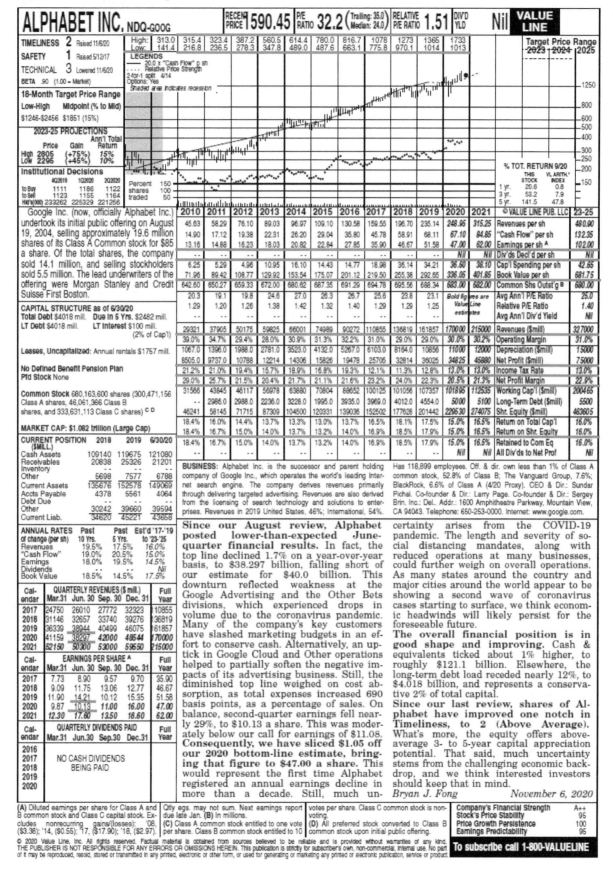

ALPHABET INC. NDQ-GOOG — RECENT PRICE 590.45 | P/E RATIO 32.2 (Trailing: 35.0 / Median: 24.0) | RELATIVE P/E RATIO 1.51 | DIV'D YLD Nil

VALUE LINE

TIMELINESS **2** Raised 11/6/20
SAFETY **1** Raised 5/12/17
TECHNICAL **3** Lowered 11/6/20
BETA .90 (1.00 = Market)

18-Month Target Price Range
Low-High   Midpoint (% to Mid)
$1246-$2456 $1851 (15%)

2023-25 PROJECTIONS
	Price	Gain	Ann'l Total Return
High	2805	(+75%)	15%
Low	2295	(+45%)	10%

Institutional Decisions
	4Q2019	1Q2020	2Q2020
to Buy	1111	1186	1122
to Sell	1123	1155	1164
Hld's(000)	233262	225329	221256

Google Inc. (now, officially Alphabet Inc.) undertook its initial public offering on August 19, 2004, selling approximately 19.6 million shares of its Class A Common stock for $85 a share. Of the total shares, the company sold 14.1 million, and selling stockholders sold 5.5 million. The lead underwriters of the offering were Morgan Stanley and Credit Suisse First Boston.

CAPITAL STRUCTURE as of 6/30/20
Total Debt $4018 mill. Due in 5 Yrs. $2482 mill.
LT Debt $4018 mill. LT Interest $100 mill.
(2% of Cap'l)

Leases, Uncapitalized: Annual rentals $1757 mill.

No Defined Benefit Pension Plan
Pfd Stock None

Common Stock 680,163,600 shares (300,471,156 Class A shares, 46,061,366 Class B shares, and 333,631,113 Class C shares) C D

MARKET CAP: $1.082 trillion (Large Cap)

CURRENT POSITION
($MILL.)	2018	2019	6/30/20
Cash Assets	109140	119675	121080
Receivables	20838	25326	21201
Inventory	--	--	--
Other	5698	7577	6788
Current Assets	135676	152578	149069
Accts Payable	4378	5561	4064
Debt Due	--	--	--
Other	30242	39660	39594
Current Liab.	34620	45221	43658

ANNUAL RATES
of change (per sh)	Past 10 Yrs.	Past 5 Yrs.	Est'd '17-'19 to '23-'25
Revenues	19.5%	17.5%	16.0%
"Cash Flow"	19.0%	20.5%	15.0%
Earnings	18.0%	19.5%	14.5%
Dividends	--	--	Nil
Book Value	18.5%	14.5%	17.5%

QUARTERLY REVENUES ($ mill.)
Cal-endar	Mar.31	Jun. 30	Sep. 30	Dec. 31	Full Year
2017	24750	26010	27772	32323	110855
2018	31146	32657	33740	39276	136819
2019	36339	38944	40499	46075	161857
2020	41159	38297	42000	48544	170000
2021	52150	50300	52500	59550	215000

EARNINGS PER SHARE A
Cal-endar	Mar.31	Jun. 30	Sep. 30	Dec. 31	Full Year
2017	7.73	8.90	9.57	9.70	35.90
2018	9.09	11.75	13.06	12.77	46.67
2019	11.90	14.21	10.12	15.35	51.58
2020	9.87	10.13	11.00	16.00	47.00
2021	12.30	17.80	13.50	62.00	62.00

QUARTERLY DIVIDENDS PAID
Cal-endar	Mar.31	Jun.30	Sep.30	Dec.31	Full Year
2016					
2017		NO CASH DIVIDENDS			
2018		BEING PAID			
2019					
2020					

	2010	2011	2012	2013	2014	2015	2016	2017	2018	2019	2020	2021	© VALUE LINE PUB. LLC	23-25
Revenues per sh	45.63	58.29	76.10	89.03	96.97	109.10	130.58	159.55	196.70	235.14	248.95	315.25	Revenues per sh	480.90
"Cash Flow" per sh	14.90	17.12	19.38	22.31	26.20	29.04	35.80	45.78	58.91	68.11	67.10	84.85	"Cash Flow" per sh	132.35
Earnings per sh A	13.16	14.88	16.23	18.03	20.82	22.84	27.85	35.90	46.67	51.58	47.00	62.00	Earnings per sh A	102.00
Div'ds Decl'd per sh	--	--	--	--	--	--	--	--	--	--	Nil	Nil	Div'ds Decl'd per sh	Nil
Cap'l Spending per sh	6.25	5.29	4.96	10.95	16.10	14.43	14.77	18.98	36.14	34.21	36.60	38.10	Cap'l Spending per sh	42.65
Book Value per sh	71.96	89.42	108.77	129.92	153.54	175.07	201.12	219.50	255.38	292.65	336.05	401.85	Book Value per sh	681.75
Common Shs Outst'g B	642.60	650.27	659.33	672.00	680.62	687.35	691.29	694.78	695.56	688.34	683.00	682.00	Common Shs Outst'g B	680.00
Avg Ann'l P/E Ratio	20.3	19.1	19.8	24.6	27.0	26.3	26.7	25.6	23.8	23.1	Bold figures are Value Line estimates		Avg Ann'l P/E Ratio	25.0
Relative P/E Ratio	1.29	1.20	1.26	1.38	1.42	1.32	1.40	1.29	1.29	1.25			Relative P/E Ratio	1.40
Avg Ann'l Div'd Yield	--	--	--	--	--	--	--	--	--	--			Avg Ann'l Div'd Yield	Nil
Revenues ($mill)	29321	37905	50175	59825	66001	74989	90272	110855	136819	161857	170000	215000	Revenues ($mill)	327000
Operating Margin	39.0%	34.7%	29.4%	28.0%	30.9%	31.3%	32.2%	31.0%	29.0%	29.0%	30.0%	30.2%	Operating Margin	31.0%
Depreciation ($mill)	1067.0	1396.0	1988.0	2781.0	3523.0	4132.0	5267.0	6103.0	8164.0	10856	11000	12000	Depreciation ($mill)	15000
Net Profit ($mill)	8505.0	9737.0	10788	12214	14306	15826	19478	25705	32914	36025	34825	45880	Net Profit ($mill)	75000
Income Tax Rate	21.2%	21.0%	19.4%	15.7%	18.9%	16.8%	19.3%	12.1%	11.3%	12.8%	13.0%	13.0%	Income Tax Rate	13.0%
Net Profit Margin	29.0%	25.7%	21.5%	20.4%	21.7%	21.1%	21.6%	23.2%	24.0%	22.3%	20.5%	21.3%	Net Profit Margin	22.9%
Working Cap'l ($mill)	31566	43845	46117	56978	63680	70804	88652	100125	101056	107357	101895	112535	Working Cap'l ($mill)	200465
Long-Term Debt ($mill)	--	2986.0	2988.0	2236.0	3228.0	1995.0	3935.0	3969.0	4012.0	4554.0	5000	5100	Long-Term Debt ($mill)	5500
Shr. Equity ($mill)	46241	58145	71715	87309	104500	120331	139036	152502	177628	201442	229530	274075	Shr. Equity ($mill)	463605
Return on Total Cap'l	18.4%	16.0%	14.4%	13.7%	13.3%	13.0%	13.7%	16.5%	18.1%	17.5%	15.0%	16.5%	Return on Total Cap'l	16.0%
Return on Shr. Equity	18.4%	16.7%	15.0%	14.0%	13.7%	13.2%	14.0%	16.9%	18.5%	17.9%	15.0%	16.5%	Return on Shr. Equity	16.0%
Retained to Com Eq	18.4%	16.7%	15.0%	14.0%	13.7%	13.2%	14.0%	16.9%	18.5%	17.9%	15.0%	16.5%	Retained to Com Eq	16.0%
All Div'ds to Net Prof	--	--	--	--	--	--	--	--	--	--	Nil	Nil	All Div'ds to Net Prof	Nil

BUSINESS: Alphabet Inc. is the successor and parent holding company of Google Inc., which operates the world's leading Internet search engine. The company derives revenues primarily through delivering targeted advertising. Revenues are also derived from the licensing of search technology and solutions to enterprises. Revenues in 2019 United States, 46%; International, 54%. Has 118,899 employees. Off. & dir. own less than 1% of Class A common stock, 52.8% of Class B; The Vanguard Group, 7.6%; BlackRock, 6.6% of Class A (4/20 Proxy). CEO & Dir.: Sundar Pichai. Co-founder & Dir.: Larry Page. Co-founder & Dir.: Sergey Brin. Inc.: Del. Addr.: 1600 Amphitheatre Parkway, Mountain View, CA 94043. Telephone: 650-253-0000. Internet: www.google.com.

Since our August review, Alphabet posted lower-than-expected June-quarter financial results. In fact, the top line declined 1.7% on a year-over-year basis, to $38.297 billion, falling short of our estimate for $40.0 billion. This downturn reflected weakness at the Google Advertising and the Other Bets divisions, which experienced drops in volume due to the coronavirus pandemic. Many of the company's key customers have slashed marketing budgets in an effort to conserve cash. Alternatively, an uptick in Google Cloud and Other operations helped to partially soften the negative impacts of its advertising business. Still, the diminished top line weighed on cost absorption, as total expenses increased 690 basis points, as a percentage of sales. On balance, second-quarter earnings fell nearly 29%, to $10.13 a share. This was moderately below our call for earnings of $11.08. Consequently, we have sliced $1.05 off our 2020 bottom-line estimate, bringing that figure to $47.00 a share. This would represent the first time Alphabet registered an annual earnings decline in more than a decade. Still, much un-

certainty arises from the COVID-19 pandemic. The length and severity of social distancing mandates, along with reduced operations at many businesses, could further weigh on overall operations. As many states around the country and major cities around the world appear to be showing a second wave of coronavirus cases starting to surface, we think economic headwinds will likely persist for the foreseeable future.
The overall financial position is in good shape and improving. Cash & equivalents ticked about 1% higher, to roughly $121.1 billion. Elsewhere, the long-term debt receded nearly 12%, to $4.018 billion, and represents a conservative 2% of total capital.
Since our last review, shares of Alphabet have improved one notch in Timeliness, to 2 (Above Average). What's more, the equity offers above-average 3- to 5-year capital appreciation potential. That said, much uncertainty stems from the challenging economic backdrop, and we think interested investors should keep that in mind.
Bryan J. Fong   *November 6, 2020*

Morningstar Fund Report

Release Date: 09-30-2020

S&P 500 Index Fund

Benchmark
S&P 500 TR USD

Investment Objective & Strategy

The investment seeks to track the performance of a benchmark index that measures the investment return of large-capitalization stocks.

The fund employs an indexing investment approach designed to track the performance of the Standard & Poor's 500 Index, a widely recognized benchmark of U.S. stock market performance that is dominated by the stocks of large U.S. companies. The advisor attempts to replicate the target index by investing all, or substantially all, of its assets in the stocks that make up the index, holding each stock in approximately the same proportion as its weighting in the index.

Operations and Management

Fund Inception Date	12-30-16
Expense Ratio	0.02%
Portfolio Manager(s)	Donald M. Butler, CFA
	Michelle Louie, CFA
Name of Issuer	Vanguard
Management Company	Vanguard Group Inc

Benchmark Description: S&P 500 TR USD

The index measures the performance of 500 widely held stocks in US equity market. Standard and Poor's chooses member companies for the index based on market size, liquidity and industry group representation. Included are the stocks of industrial, financial, utility, and transportation companies. Since mid 1989, this composition has been more flexible and the number of issues in each sector has varied. It is market capitalization-weighted.

Category Description: Large Blend

Large-blend portfolios are fairly representative of the overall US stock market in size, growth rates and price. Stocks in the top 70% of the capitalization of the US equity market are defined as large cap. The blend style is assigned to portfolios where neither growth nor value characteristics predominate. These portfolios tend to invest across the spectrum of US industries, and owing to their broad exposure, the portfolios' returns are often similar to those of the S&P 500 Index.

Volatility Analysis

In the past, this investment has shown a relatively moderate range of price fluctuations relative to other investments. This investment may experience larger or smaller price declines or price increases depending on market conditions. Some of this risk may be offset by owning other investments with different portfolio makeups or investment strategies.

Performance

	QTD	YTD	1 Year	3 Year	5 Year	10 Year	Since Inception
Fund Return %	8.95	5.57	15.14	12.27	14.14	13.74	6.78
Benchmark Return %	8.93	5.57	15.15	12.28	14.15	13.74	6.75
Category Average %	8.06	2.30	10.70	9.55	11.77	11.96	5.53
# of Funds in Category	1,448	1,387	1,370	1,229	1,066	819	—

Calendar Year Total Returns	2020	2019	2018	2017	2016	2015	2014	2013	2012	2011
Total Return %	5.57	31.49	-4.41	21.81	11.95	1.39	13.68	32.37	16.00	2.11
Benchmark Return %	5.57	31.49	-4.38	21.83	11.96	1.38	13.69	32.39	16.00	2.11
Category Average %	2.30	28.78	-6.27	20.44	10.37	-1.07	10.96	31.50	14.96	-1.27
# of Funds in Category	1387	1387	1402	1396	1409	1606	1568	1559	1686	1786

Performance Disclosure: The performance data quoted represents past performance and does not guarantee future results. The investment return and principal value of an investment will fluctuate; thus an investor's shares, when redeemed, may be worth more or less than their original cost. Current Month performance may be higher or lower than return data quoted herein. For more current information including month-end performance, please visit Oxy.voya.com or call the Oxy Retirement Service Center at 1-844-OXY-401K (1-844-699-4015). Please refer to the performance section of the disclosure page for more information.

Portfolio Analysis as of 09-30-20

Composition as of 09-30-20

	% Assets
● U.S. Stocks	98.5
● Non-U.S. Stocks	0.9
● Bonds	0.0
● Cash	0.6
● Other	0.0

Morningstar Equity Style Box™ as of 09-30-20

	% Mkt Cap
Giant	52.88
Large	34.28
Medium	12.68
Small	0.17
Micro	0.00

Top 10 Holdings as of 09-30-20

	% Assets
Apple Inc	6.65
Microsoft Corp	5.68
Amazon.com Inc	4.79
Facebook Inc A	2.25
Alphabet Inc A	1.57
Alphabet Inc Class C	1.54
Berkshire Hathaway Inc Class B	1.48
Johnson & Johnson	1.40
Procter & Gamble Co	1.24
Visa Inc Class A	1.20
Total Number of Stock Holdings	508
Total Number of Bond Holdings	2
Annual Turnover Ratio %	4.00
Total Fund Assets ($mil)	422.14

Morningstar Equity Sectors as of 09-30-20

	% Fund	S&P 500 %
℧ Cyclical	29.02	29.03
Basic Materials	2.26	2.27
Consumer Cyclical	11.32	11.31
Financial Services	12.80	12.81
Real Estate	2.64	2.64
⩗ Sensitive	46.20	46.17
Communication Services	10.80	10.80
Energy	2.05	2.06
Industrials	8.63	8.62
Technology	24.72	24.69
→ Defensive	24.79	24.79
Consumer Defensive	7.50	7.50
Healthcare	14.33	14.32
Utilities	2.96	2.97

Principal Risks as of 09-30-20

Loss of Money, Not FDIC Insured, Market/Market Volatility, Equity Securities, ETF, Early Close/Late Close/Trading Halt, Management, Market Trading

The domestic stock market is an investment cornucopia that offers shares of about 3,600 public companies for sale. But, this overwhelming variety actually pales in comparison to the 38,000 products sold at an average chain grocery store. Supermarket food products are typically organized into about ten departments such as dairy, meat, and produce as shown in the table below. Each department is subdivided further into smaller categories such as dairy (butter, cheese, and yogurt), meat (beef, chicken, and pork), and produce (fruits and vegetables). Each subcategory includes specific brand name products such as yogurt (Dannon, Yoplait, and Chobani), soft drinks (Coke, Pepsi, and Dr. Pepper), and fruit (Chaquita bananas, Dole pineapples, and Sunkist oranges).

SUPERMARKET FOOD DEPARTMENTS									
Bakery	Beverages	Bulk Foods	Dairy	Deli	Frozen Food	Meat	Packaged Foods	Produce	Seafood
Bagels	Beer	Barley	Butter	Bacon	Fruits	Beef	Cereal	Apples	Cod
Bread	Cider	Nuts	Cheese	Cole Slaw	Ice Cream	Chicken	Condiments	Bananas	Crab
Cake	Distilled Spirits	Oatmeal	Cottage Cheese	Corned Beef	Pizza	Duck	Jelly	Carrots	Halibut
Cookies	Juices	Popcorn	Cream Cheese	Ham	Vegetables	Goat	Olive Oil	Corn	Lobster
Muffins	Soft Drinks	Raisins	Eggs	Lox	Waffles	Lamb	Pasta	Oranges	Salmon
Pastries	Water	Rice	Milk	Pastrami		Pork	Peanut Butter	Pineapple	Shrimp
Pie	Wine	Seeds	Sour Cream	Pickles		Turkey	Soup	Potatoes	Tilapia
		Wheat	Whipped Cream	Salads		Veal	Spices	Spinach	Trout
			Yogurt	Salami			Tomato Sauce	Strawberries	
				Sausage			Vinegar	Tomatoes	

People shop for food each week, find all the ingredients they want, and incorporate them into the meals that define their diet. And every single person has their own successful strategy to get the food required to stay alive. Most people are so familiar with the supermarket, they no longer think twice about it.

Similarly, the stock market universe can be organized into eleven economic sectors (including real estate), which comprise 69 industries. These, in turn, include 3,600 individual companies. For example, Value Line classifies Intel, NVIDIA, and Texas Instruments all as technology sector, semiconductor industry companies. Amazon, Facebook, and Alphabet (Google) are technology sector, internet (IT services) industry companies. Morningstar lists the proportion of assets from each economic sector and also the top companies held in a fund. Technology, Health Care, Financials, Consumer Discretionary, and Communication Services comprise 74% of the S&P 500.

STOCK MARKET SECTORS AND INDUSTRIES					
CYCLICAL: $\beta > 1$		SENSITIVE: $\beta \sim 1$		DEFENSIVE: $\beta < 1$	
Materials	Consumer Discretionary	Energy	Industrials	Consumer Staples	Health Care
Chemicals	Auto Components	Energy Equipment & Services	Aerospace & Defense	Food & Staples Retailing	Health Care Equip. & Supplies
Construction Materials	Automobiles	Oil, Gas & Consumable Fuels	Building Products	Beverages	Health Care Providers & Services
Containers & Packaging	Household Durables		Construction & Engineering	Food Products	Health Care Technology
Metals & Mining	Leisure Products	**Information Technology**	Electrical Equipment	Tobacco	Biotechnology
Paper & Forest Products	Textiles, Apparel & Luxury Goods	IT Services	Industrial Conglomerates	Household Products	Pharmaceuticals
	Hotels, Restaurants & Leisure	Software	Machinery	Personal Products	Life Sciences Tools & Services
Financials	Diversified Consumer Services	Communications Equipment	Trading Companies & Distributors		
Banks	Distributors	Tech Hardware & Storage	Commercial Services & Supplies	**Utilities**	
Thrifts & Mortgage Finance	Internet & Direct Marketing Retail	Electronic Equip. & Instruments	Professional Services	Electric Utilities	
Diversified Financial Services	Multiline Retail	Semiconductors & Equipment	Air Freight & Logistics	Gas Utilities	
Consumer Finance	Specialty Retail		Airlines	Multi-Utilities	
Capital Markets		**Communication Services**	Marine	Water Utilities	
Mortgage REITs	**Real Estate**	Diversified Telecom Services	Road & Rail	Independent & Renewable Power	
Insurance	Equity REITs	Wireless Telecom Services	Transportation Infrastructure		
	Real Estate Mgmt. & Devel.	Media			
		Entertainment			
		Interactive Media & Services			

β is the risk-free return of an individual investment divided by its market benchmark return (e.g. S&P 500 index) - i.e. **investment sensitivity**

One viable strategy at this market would be to add one of each item from every aisle in all departments to your shopping cart. You simply buy a share of the entire store. ***Total market stock funds take this blanket approach.***

The strategy could be refined to include only the top 500 biggest and best items instead. A mutual fund or ETF designed to track the S&P 500 index suits this objective (VOO). Confine your shopping to cover one department in a single purchase by choosing a sector fund. Drill deeper with a fund that excludes all but one or two industries. Or pick individual stocks from selected industries and sectors to build your portfolio from the bottom up despite the extra effort and risk. The right ingredients depend on your own recipe for financial success.

In contrast to the Value Line approach of characterizing stocks by sector and industry, Morningstar classifies a stock fund by its composite companies' size and style.

Fund Investment Style

Value	Blend	Growth	
			Size Large
			Mid
			Small

Large-cap stocks account for 70% of all market value, mid-cap stocks total 20%, and small-cap stocks make up the remaining 10%. Although the size boundaries may shift with the market, large companies have a market capitalization over $8 billion to $10 billion. Small companies have a market capitalization under $800 million to $1 billion. The market cap of a stock is its current price times the number of shares outstanding.

A growth stock is characterized by high historical growth of earnings, sales, cash flow, and book value. The projected long-term earnings growth is relatively high as well. A value stock is distinguished by low historical price to book, sales, and cash flow ratios and perhaps a high dividend yield. The price to projected earnings ratio is also relatively low. A stock whose value and growth attributes are comparable is considered a blend. Value, Blend, and Growth stock styles each account for about one-third of all market value.

When you buy common stock, you implicitly pay for two things claimed by that company: its present assets and future earnings stream. Money in the bank now and more money anticipated to come in the future are related since assets are basically accumulated earnings. A growth stock emphasizes its future earnings stream. The price history of a true growth stock resembles the growth plot previously shown. In contrast, a value stock features its assets and/or cyclical growth. The price history of a value stock looks more like the equilibrium plot.

4.2 Unit Pricing for Stocks - The Price to Earnings Ratio

The price to earnings ratio (P/E) states how much an investor pays for $1 of earnings per year in return. Thus, the P/E is one measure of an investment's value, i.e. how hard that investment works. For example, consider the two following investments. Investment A costs $100 and earns $5 in one year. This investment has an earnings yield of $5 divided by $100, i.e., 5%. The P/E ratio is $100 divided by $5, that is, 20. In comparison, investment B costs $100 and returns $10 in one year. This investment has an earnings yield of 10% and a P/E ratio of 10. Thus, investment B is a better value because it earns twice as much as investment A for the same price. In other words, investment B costs half as much for the same earnings. Half of knowing what you really want is knowing what you must give up to get it.

Investment A		Investment B	
$100 outlay	Returns $5 in one year	$100 outlay	Returns $10 in one year
Price = $100	Earnings = $5	Price = $100	Earnings = $10
Earnings yield = Earnings / Price = $5 / $100 = 0.05 or 5%		Earnings yield = Earnings / Price = $10 / $100 = 0.10 or 10%	
P / E ratio = Price / Earnings = $100 / $5 = 20		P / E ratio = Price / Earnings = $100 / $10 = 10	

To fully comprehend the price to earnings ratio, consider your supermarket shopping experience once again. Is $2.19 a fair price to pay for rice at the store? Is that a good deal? The answer depends on a key missing factor. You can't judge the transaction until you know how much rice was received in return for the cash. A three-pound package would certainly be worth more than a one-pound package. The size matters. Weight classes were established long ago for Olympic wrestlers and boxers to ensure a fair contest. The command to "pick on someone your own size" officially became a mandate.

Every financial transaction is an agreement between a buyer and a seller to exchange an asset for payment. The price alone stipulates only half of the agreement, the payment amount. The package size quantifies the other half, the asset amount. *The transaction choice is clear only once the payment and the goods are both explicit.* These terms are displayed at grocery stores for your shopping convenience today as unit prices. Some specific examples are shown in the figure below.

A Price / Earnings Ratio Analogy
A Portfolio of Groceries

Food comes in different size packages, but a fair price comparison requires each package to be the same size. Food is generally compared on a weight basis, that is, the price per pound. Unit prices, first introduced in North America around 1973, help consumers quickly identify the best purchase and realize significant savings. [Wikipedia, ref 13] *Never buy merchandise (or an investment) without knowing how much you get in return.*

Companies also come in different size portions or shares. Company shares are typically compared based on annual earnings, that is, price per dollar earned in a year. ***So, the P/E ratio is simply the unit price for stocks.*** The table below compares stocks based on their unit prices. The P/E ratio is the proper starting point to debate the value of stock market merchandise. Multiplying the P/E ratio by the current (trailing twelve months) or anticipated future earnings/share gives a corresponding price/share. Thus, the P/E ratio is also called the "P/E multiple" or just "multiple" for short.

Unit Price View of Assorted Stocks (December 2020)

Ticker	Growth Rate	Price/Share	Earn/Share	P/E
AAPL	17.4%	132.69	3.28	40.5
ADBE	19.5%	500.12	7.94	63.0
AMT	6.9%	217.40	4.23	51.4
AMZN	25.4%	3256.93	32.63	99.8
APD	5.0%	273.22	8.38	32.6
BLK	11.0%	721.54	32.01	22.5
BSX	14.3%	35.56	0.82	43.4
COST	11.0%	376.48	9.38	40.1
DG	14.2%	210.30	10.09	20.8
FB	15.7%	273.16	7.87	34.7
GOOG	16.8%	1751.88	51.75	33.9
HAS	6.7%	92.75	3.71	25.0
HD	13.7%	265.62	11.56	23.0
HON	11.2%	212.70	7.09	30.0
JNJ	4.1%	157.38	8.05	19.6
MSFT	6.7%	222.42	6.19	35.9
NEE	5.6%	77.15	1.98	39.0
NFLX	17.3%	540.73	6.2	87.2
PLD	11.3%	99.66	2.56	38.9
SHW	14.4%	734.91	23.74	31.0
TDG	14.1%	618.85	8.14	76.0
TDOC	N/A	199.96	-1.43	N/A
TMO	8.5%	465.78	12.2	38.2
UNH	15.1%	350.68	18.25	19.2
UNP	11.4%	208.22	7.78	26.8
VZ	3.1%	58.75	4.82	12.2
WEC	6.5%	90.55	3.8	23.8
WMT	0.7%	144.15	5.28	27.3

Note: no earnings yet for TDOC means unit price does not yet apply!

Although a lower unit price indicates less expensive merchandise, buyers may perceive other benefits that might justify spending more on a purchase. Safety and growth are two reasons that otherwise sensible investors could actually prefer a higher P/E investment. For example, safety would be paramount to a retiree with a tight budget. If Investment A earnings were a sure bet, but Investment B earnings were groundless speculation, peace of mind might justify choosing Investment A despite its higher unit price. In nursery school terms, if you don't actually receive a two marshmallow reward each time, then you might decide to accept a lesser reward you can truly count on. Growth would be important to a recent college graduate with a new 401(k) retirement plan. The previous Investment A and B comparison used a single snapshot in time, but a more comprehensive evaluation (such as a discounted cash flow calculation) would be based on several sequential snapshots instead. For instance, Investment A would seem better if it returned $5 the first year, $10 the second year, $15 the third year, $20 the fourth year, and $25 the fifth year, while Investment B returned just $10 every single year. So, waiting for just one marshmallow instead of two the first time would be OK in nursery school if the reward came with an extra marshmallow each successive time after that.

A supermarket shopper intuitively compares the benefits of fresh salmon priced at $9.99/pound relative to ground beef priced at $3.99/pound. An investor can compare the benefits of a faster growing company with a higher P/E ratio stock relative to a lower P/E ratio stock by using the PEG ratio. To calculate its value for each stock, simply divide the P/E ratio by the percent annual earnings growth rate. Although the PEG ratio declares nothing about the certainty of the projected earnings growth, it does assert that faster growing earnings warrant a higher investment P/E. The PEG ratio is not meant to stand alone, but to rank alternative investments relative to each other at a specific time. Fidelity Magellan mutual fund manager Peter Lynch made the PEG ratio popular in the 1980 s. [ref 14]

The figure below shows the previously listed stock P/E ratios versus their earnings growth rates. Low P/E stocks with relatively high growth rates depict bargain merchandise at a clearance sale (advantage: buyer). In contrast, high P/E stocks with lower growth rates resemble extravagant goods in an auction bidding war (advantage: seller). Buying a stock with no earnings yet is like purchasing an orchard before its trees bear any fruit at all. *"Growth At a Reasonable Price" (GARP) is a universal investment motto.*

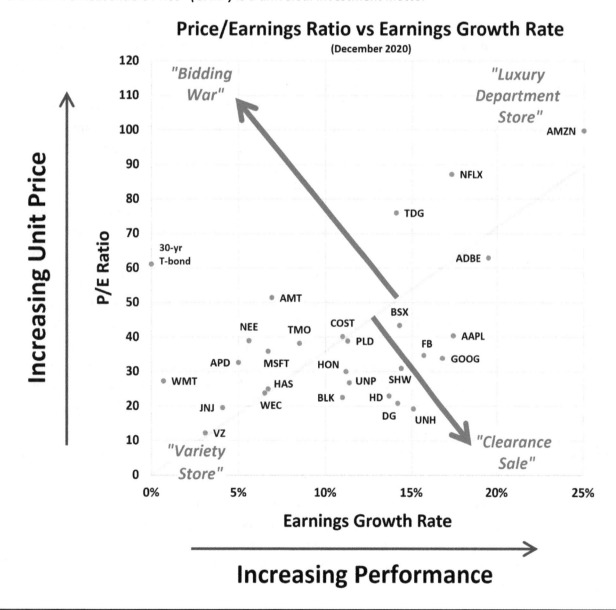

In addition to expected earnings, stock P/E ratios ultimately depend on another fundamental factor, namely interest rates. [Lowenstein, ref 15] For example, in November 1985, the 30-year United States Treasury bond yield was 10% per year. Just like the Investment B example previously mentioned, this amounts to a P/E ratio of 10. At that time, the S&P 500 stock index earnings yield was roughly 7.5%, equivalent to a P/E ratio of about 13. So, investors had the choice of a relatively safe bet that returned 10% each year with no growth or a relatively more expensive investment with less consistent but potentially faster growing future returns. Annual inflation was then 3.5%. [Schiller, ref 16]

Years later, in November 2001, the 30-year US T-bond yield was 5% per year. Like investment A, this represents a P/E ratio of 20. The S&P 500 stock index earnings yield then was only 2.25%, equivalent to a P/E of about 44. Annual inflation had dropped to 1.75%. The investment choice had become a relatively safe bet that returned 5% each year with no growth versus paying twice the unit price for an alternate investment with legitimate growth prospects. In December 2020, the S&P 500 earnings yield was 2.7% (P/E = 37). The 30-yr T-bond yield was 1.65% (P/E = 61). Inflation was just 1.2%. Investors chose stocks because "There Is No Alternative" (TINA).

So, US Treasury bonds provide a relatively safe return of interest in contrast to stocks that generate earnings with more growth potential. Because bonds and stocks both compete for investors' capital, interest rates significantly influence stock P/E ratios in the long term. When interest rates drop, stock earnings become more valuable compared to less interest offered by US Treasury bonds. In addition, lower interest payments on borrowed money make a business more profitable by reducing costs. Consequently, P/E ratios usually increase, and stock prices rise. When interest rates rise, stock earnings become less valuable by comparison, business borrowing costs increase to reduce profits, and P/E ratios decrease. Stock prices drop accordingly.

4.3 Fundamental Analysis - The Business Assets & Earnings

From a fundamental view, a stock's price depends primarily on the intrinsic value of the company's business. Consequently, if and when that business becomes more valuable in the future, its stock price will rise. Fundamental analysis aims to assess the business health, evaluate management, determine the current fair value, and make financial forecasts based on the company, its industry, and the overall economy.

If you intended to buy a stake in a local private business, you would first study its history, evaluate the talent and character of its management, and learn the factors that made it profitable. You would investigate any potential competitors who could take away your customers or drive you out of business. You would emphasize the most profitable opportunities destined to stay that way permanently. If you found just one business with perpetual profits and trustworthy people, you'd feel lucky. If you found several such firms, you'd be set for life.

And once you had invested, you'd review your profits or earnings to measure your progress. If the business made more money each year, you would be happy since your share was steadily increasing. It wouldn't matter what the stock market did each day, who was president, what happened to interest rates, or even if there was a recession as long as your steady profit stream prevailed.

To quote Warren Buffett once again, "***The basic ideas of investing are to look at stocks as businesses, use the market's fluctuations to your advantage, and seek a margin of safety.*** That's what Ben Graham taught us. A hundred years from now they will still be the cornerstones of investing."   Buffet's approach is summarized in detail by 12 investment tenets on the following page that specifically question the business, its management, finances, and value. [Hagstrom, ref 17]

THE WARREN BUFFETT WAY

Business Tenets

1. Is the business simple and understandable?
2. Does the business have a consistent operating history?
3. Does the business have favorable long-term prospects?

Management Tenets

4. Is management rational?
5. Is management candid with its shareholders?
6. Does management resist the institutional imperative?

Financial Tenets

7. What is the return on equity?
8. What are the company's "owner earnings"?
9. What are the profit margins?
10. Has the company created at least one dollar of market value for every dollar retained?

Value Tenets

11. What is the value of the company?
12. Can it be purchased at a significant discount to its value?

Stocks are now routinely screened based on their fundamental financial attributes, but this is only a first step. One example of a more complete fundamental approach is the BetterInvesting Stock Selection Guide (SSG). The SSG was originally a two-page form devised by The National Association of Investors Corporation (NAIC) to help investors identify growth companies that could be profitable investments. [McLane, ref 18] *By definition, a growth company has sales and earnings that increase faster than the overall economy.*

The SSG uses up to ten years of annual data as input: the high price, low price, earnings/share, dividends/share, book value/share, sales, net profit, and income tax rate. Sales and earnings/share for the current quarter and the same quarter one year earlier are also considered. These figures are all found on the Value Line stock report or similar sources. (See page 19 red underlined data.) NAIC commissioned SSG stock analysis software in 1991.

SSG section 1 is a visual analysis of sales, earnings, and stock prices plotted together to show if the proposed investment (Alphabet Inc.) has been a consistent growth company. This plot provides the basis to forecast future sales and earnings that ultimately drive the price higher even though past performance never guarantees future results. The investigation ends here when the historical data is erratic, incomplete, or simply not compelling enough to inspire the leap of faith that asserts future profit growth will continue without compromise. "Study the past if you would divine the future." - Confucius

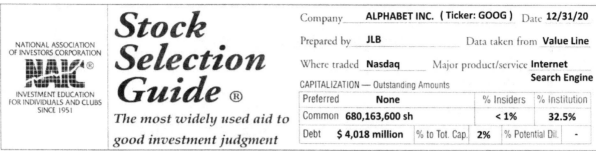

NATIONAL ASSOCIATION
OF INVESTORS CORPORATION

NAIC ®

INVESTMENT EDUCATION
FOR INDIVIDUALS AND CLUBS
SINCE 1951

Stock Selection Guide ®

The most widely used aid to good investment judgment

Company	**ALPHABET INC.** (Ticker: GOOG)	Date **12/31/20**
Prepared by	**JLB**	Data taken from **Value Line**
Where traded **Nasdaq**	Major product/service **Internet Search Engine**	

CAPITALIZATION — Outstanding Amounts

Preferred	**None**		% Insiders	% Institution
Common	**680,163,600 sh**		**< 1%**	**32.5%**
Debt	**$ 4,018 million**	% to Tot. Cap. **2%**	% Potential Dil.	**-**

1 VISUAL ANALYSIS of Sales, Earnings and Price

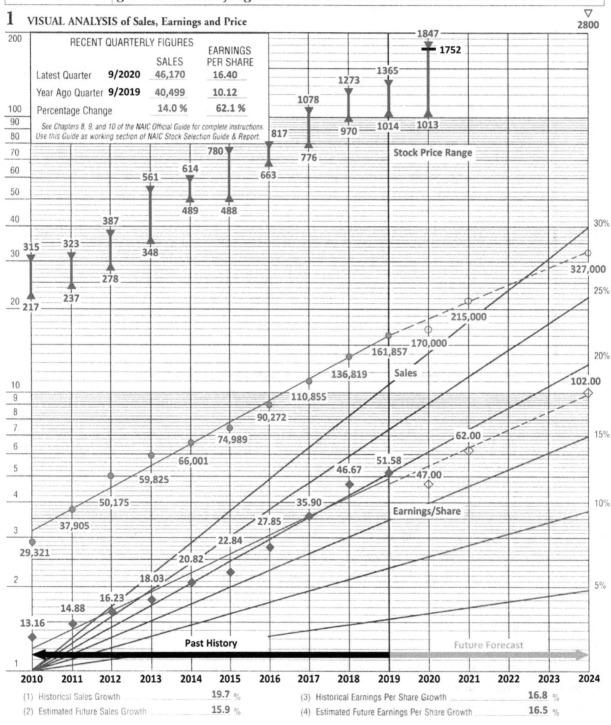

RECENT QUARTERLY FIGURES

		SALES	EARNINGS PER SHARE
Latest Quarter	9/2020	46,170	16.40
Year Ago Quarter	9/2019	40,499	10.12
Percentage Change		14.0 %	62.1 %

See Chapters 8, 9, and 10 of the NAIC Official Guide for complete instructions.
Use this Guide as working section of NAIC Stock Selection Guide & Report.

Stock Price Range

Sales

Earnings/Share

Past History

Future Forecast

(1) Historical Sales Growth .... **19.7** %
(2) Estimated Future Sales Growth **15.9** %
(3) Historical Earnings Per Share Growth .... **16.8** %
(4) Estimated Future Earnings Per Share Growth **16.5** %

SSG section 2 evaluates profit margin and return on equity trends to determine if historical growth was due to smart management instead of temporary good fortune. Deteriorating trends often foreshadow financial problems that can subvert future profitability. Look for a better competitor if this hurdle is not met.

2 EVALUATING MANAGEMENT   Company   ALPHABET INC. (Ticker: GOOG)   12/31/20

	2010	2011	2012	2013	2014	2015	2016	2017	2018	2019	LAST 5 YEAR AVG.	TREND UP	TREND DOWN
A % Pre-tax Profit on Sales (Net Before Taxes ÷ Sales)	36.8	32.5	26.7	24.2	26.8	25.4	26.8	26.4	27.1	25.6	26.2	—	
B % Earned on Equity (E/S ÷ Book Value)	18.4	16.7	15.0	14.0	13.7	13.2	14.0	16.9	18.5	17.9	16.1	↑	

SSG sections 3 to 5 determine if the price is right. Even a great business is a lousy investment when the price is too high. Section 3 is the price and earnings history used to check if the stock is now a fair deal (relative value).

3 PRICE-EARNINGS HISTORY as an indicator of the future

This shows how stock prices have fluctuated with earnings and dividends. It is a building block for translating earnings into future stock prices.

PRESENT PRICE **1751.88**   HIGH THIS YEAR **1847.20**   LOW THIS YEAR **1013.54**

Year	A PRICE HIGH	B PRICE LOW	C Earnings Per Share	D Price Earnings Ratio HIGH A÷C	E Price Earnings Ratio LOW B÷C	F Dividend Per Share	G % Payout F÷C X 100	H % High Yield F÷B X 100
1 2015	780	488	22.84	34.2	21.3	0		
2 2016	817	663	27.85	29.3	23.8	0		
3 2017	1078	776	35.90	30.0	21.6	0		
4 2018	1273	970	46.67	27.3	20.8	0		
5 2019	1365	1014	51.58	26.5	19.7	0		
6 TOTAL			Last 12 months					
7 AVERAGE	1063	782	51.75	29.4	21.4			
8 AVERAGE PRICE EARNINGS RATIO = 25.4			9 CURRENT PRICE EARNINGS RATIO = 33.9		Relative Value = 33.9 / 25.4 = 133%			

Section 4 evaluates the investment risk and reward by forecasting a high and a low price, dividing that price range into buy, hold, and sell zones, and computing the upside to downside ratio from the current price.

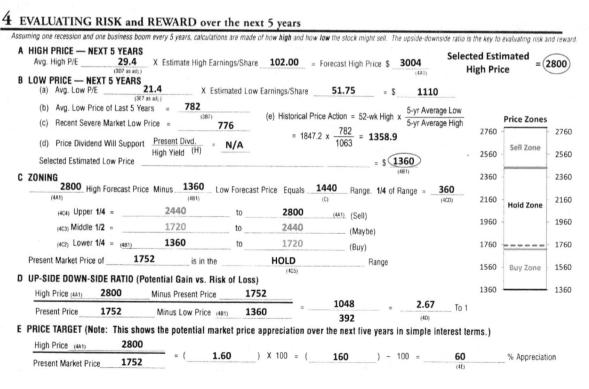

Section 5 figures the 5-year investment return by combining the forecast capital appreciation with the average dividend yield. If sections 3 to 5 indicate the price is now wrong, wait for a better transaction price to come.

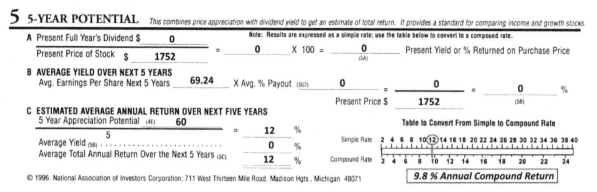

Total return is the universal standard for comparing different investment types. Yield is the periodic rent paid to use an asset owned by someone else. Examples include savings account or bond interest, real estate rent, and stock dividends. Selling an investment for a higher price than originally paid is called capital appreciation. This includes real estate and stock sales. Growth stocks stress price appreciation; value stocks often emphasize the dividend. Total return is the yield plus the capital appreciation, both based on the same time period.

The Stock Selection Guide recommends investing in stocks that meet the following criteria:

Section 1) Consistent sales and earnings growth for at least 5 years
Section 2) Profit margins and return on equity both increasing or holding steady above industry average
Section 3) Relative value (current P/E divided by historical average P/E) between 80% and 110%
Section 4) Current price in the "BUY" zone and Upside/Downside ratio at least 3:1
Section 5) Forecast total return (dividend yield + price appreciation) 15% or more compounded annually

The SSG is more than just a cookbook number-crunching exercise. It is your guide to learning the business behind a public company's stock. No fundamental analysis is ever truly complete until you hear someone else confirm the story you learned based on this simple test:

If you can't explain to your parents and your children in plain English how a specific business makes money and why that business will be worth more in the future, you need to finish your research BEFORE you invest.

Investment opportunities are repeatedly disguised as debates between sellers expressing fear and buyers expressing greed. A profitable, growing business driven by sound management and acquired at a fair price often proves to be a good investment, but not always. Nothing is a sure bet. Once you identify a promising opportunity, figure out why this seemingly great investment now trades at a bargain P/E ratio. For example, consider several potential reasons listed below.

1) The whole market is on sale   *5) Competition presents a new threat*
2) The whole sector is on sale   *6) Key business partner is lost*
3) The whole industry is on sale   *7) Fundamental problem is permanent damage*
4) Recent performance and/or forecast blemish *8) Executive management change*

The more specific the reason is to this business, the more careful you should be. The more persistent the reason is, the more skeptical you should be. Use the SSG to develop and exercise good judgment so you won't be fooled by tortured numbers that confess a story too good to be true.

___

CHAPTER 5

5) MONEY & RISK MANAGEMENT: Limit the Size of Each Investment

A buy-and-hold investor who acquires fundamentally sound assets may not need to sell for many years. Still, even a great investment may ultimately fail. And that could spell disaster especially if it occurs just before your retirement horizon. For example, the stock price chart below shows that General Electric was an exceptional investment that grew from $2/share in 1990 to $31/share in 2000. However, GE has languished ever since then even though it might recover again from $6/share. But, other shooting stars were not so fortunate. Companies such as Enron, Lehman Brothers, and WorldCom are now gone forever. Investors who held their whole fortune in any single one of these stocks were completely wiped out. Even fully invested S&P 500 index fund devotees lost half their portfolio value twice between 2000 and 2010. Each time, a full recovery took five years.

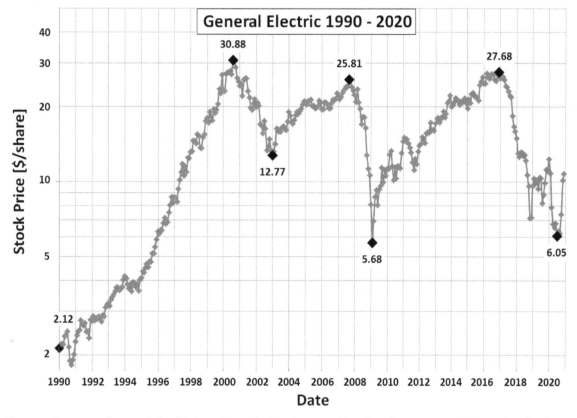

Risk is like running out of gas while driving through the desert. Plan for the worst and hope for the best. Every investor suffers losing trades. If you put all your eggs in one basket, you risk losing them all at once. But, you can proactively choose to avoid tragic setbacks. Keep losses relatively small so you can weather a bad streak and still stay in the game. It is much easier to recover from a mosquito bite than a failed parachute. *So, before you buy any investment, always focus on how much you could lose first instead of how much you might gain*. Limit your risk before your investment can go south.

The first decision you need to make in advance is when to sell and cut your loss if the price of your investment has dropped significantly and shows no signs of turning around. This tactic is called money management. The second decision you must make is even more important, namely, how much of your entire portfolio you would tolerate losing on any single investment. This tactic is called risk management. Together, these two decisions determine the size of each and every investment in your whole portfolio. [Nyaradi, 19] You deliberately buy a limited amount of each specific investment so that its failure does not cripple you.

Your money and risk management may ultimately determine your success or failure as much as finding the right investment to buy or the right time to buy it. Money management defines the point where you admit your investment went wrong; you cut losers fast and let winners run. It is better to miss a profit than take a loss. The pain from a loss feels twice as powerful as the pleasure from a gain. Risk management defines the consequence you accept whenever you are wrong; you set your own Skinner box penalty for every investment.

For example, a professionally managed portfolio of individual stocks (and bonds) may limit the maximum loss per trade to be 1% of the whole portfolio. So, if you lost 100% of your investment in stock of a company that went bankrupt, but you still had equal amounts of stock in 99 other successful companies, you have limited the damage. If you lost 10% of your investment in stock you held in a company that suffered permanent lost business, but you still had equal amounts of stock in 9 other successful companies, you have also limited the overall damage to 1%. Your stake in the lost business company was 10% of all your money and you lost 10% of that stake. Your stake in the bankrupt company was only 1% of your money and you lost 100% of that stake. *So, take a smaller stake in more risky investments that could lose more.*

You may stubbornly insist that your investment could still turn around and hold it until it was worthless, but you should react to trouble much sooner. At the other extreme, you could sell after the price dropped just 1%, only to miss a big gain after a reversal. Therefore, you should also leave enough breathing room for routine price fluctuations. You need a leash on every investment so when it strays too far off course, you feel a tug. A steady, well-behaved investment runs on a shorter leash without pulling compared to a jittery, less obedient investment that meanders more widely.

For instance, you might choose to stop the loss on a small-cap, pharmaceutical stock at 13% of your original investment. In contrast, you might decide to sell a short-term U.S. Treasury bond fund to stop your loss at just 5%. Study the price variance history (e.g. five-year standard deviation of quarterly returns) of each investment to help set its money management stop loss point. A stop loss order is free insurance that acts like a circuit breaker. It will automatically sell your investment for cash when the price drops to any low point you choose.

Once you have decided how you will manage your money and risk, figuring the right amount to invest is straightforward. Simply divide your maximum portfolio risk by the investment's stop loss point to quantify the maximum percentage of your portfolio to invest in each asset.

Position Size = (% Portfolio Risk per Trade / % Stop-Loss per Trade)

Therefore, if you limit your portfolio risk to 1% and set your stop loss point at 13%, then your small-cap stock investment should be no more than 7.7% of your whole portfolio.

Position Size = (1%/ 13%) = 7.7%

So, if your portfolio totals $100,000, you allocate $7,700 on this stock purchase. That means you buy at most 100 shares if the stock price is $77 per share. You then sell to cut your losses and limit the damage if it turns out you were wrong and the price drops to $67 per share. Your loss would be 100 x ($77 - $67) = $1,000.

Similarly, if your portfolio risk is 1% and your stop loss point is 5%, then your U.S. Treasury bond fund investment should be no more than 20% of your whole portfolio.

Position Size = (1%/ 5%) = 20%

If your portfolio totals $100,000, you allocate $20,000 on this purchase. That means you buy at most 1,000 shares if the fund price is $20 per share. You then sell to cut your losses if it turns out the price drops to $19 per share. Your loss would be 1000 x ($20 - $19) = $1,000.

Not all portfolios warrant the same risk. You might take on more risk if your portfolio is small and you are more aggressive or less risk if your portfolio is large and you are conservative. The table below details the maximum position size for any portfolio risk between 0.5% and 2.5% based on any stop loss between 5% and 13%. Note that lower risk levels always mean smaller position sizes for any specific stop loss value. In addition, higher stop loss values always mean smaller position sizes for the same level of risk.

Maximum Position Size based on Portfolio Risk & Stop Loss Point						
		Risk Management				
		0.5% Risk	1% Risk	1.5% Risk	2% Risk	2.5% Risk
Money Management	5% Stop Loss	10.0%	20.0%	30.0%	40.0%	50.0%
	6% Stop Loss	8.3%	16.7%	25.0%	33.3%	41.7%
	7% Stop Loss	7.1%	14.3%	21.4%	28.6%	35.7%
	8% Stop Loss	6.3%	12.5%	18.8%	25.0%	31.3%
	9% Stop Loss	5.6%	11.1%	16.7%	22.2%	27.8%
	10% Stop Loss	5.0%	*10.0%*	15.0%	20.0%	25.0%
	11% Stop Loss	4.5%	9.1%	13.6%	18.2%	22.7%
	12% Stop Loss	4.2%	8.3%	*12.5%*	16.7%	20.8%
	13% Stop Loss	*3.8%*	7.7%	11.5%	15.4%	19.2%

———————— More Aggressive ————————▶

So, a conservative investor could construct a portfolio of 26 small-cap stocks and limit the overall risk per trade to 0.5% because each position is just 3.8% and is sold if and when it drops 13% below the purchase price. If a more aggressive investor held just 8 small-cap stocks each with a 12% stop loss point, the risk per trade triples to 1.5% mainly because each position is now 12.5%. You could allocate 10% of your portfolio to 10 different stock sector funds each with a stop loss set at 10% and your risk per trade would be 1%.

Although diversification cannot totally eliminate portfolio risk, the dangers unique to a single company, industry, or sector can be mitigated by balancing several different ones. A single company stock inherently has more risk than a group of several stocks from the same industry. Likewise, a single industry fund is riskier than a fund of several industries within the same sector. Similarly, a sector fund comes with more risk than another fund that has companies from different sectors. *Limit your maximum investment in a single company to 5% and a single sector to 15% of your whole portfolio to effectively minimize risk*. Diverse investments complement each other like different clothes from your wardrobe that cover you in any weather whatever the season.

Suppose that a portfolio now includes the investment assets listed on the next page. The portfolio risk posed by each investment is its stop loss point times the position size. This portfolio holds 10% cash and is 90% invested, but the total loss is limited to just 8.4%. Notice that if an investment is never sold under any circumstance, its stop loss point would be 100%. So, when all investments are held forever, the maximum total portfolio loss is limited only by the cash position size. Without any cash, it is indeed possible to lose the entire portfolio.

INVESTMENT DESCRIPTION	POSITION SIZE	STOP LOSS	PORTFOLIO RISK
U.S. Small-cap Growth	22.3%	8.7%	1.9%
U.S. Small-cap Value	12.8%	11.7%	1.5%
U.S. Biotech Healthcare Sector	11.1%	11.3%	1.3%
U.S. Mid-cap Blend	9.4%	9.5%	0.9%
U.S. Large-cap Blend	7.8%	12.0%	0.9%
Foreign Large Value Developed Markets	9.0%	7.7%	0.7%
Foreign Diversified Emerging Markets	5.3%	13.2%	0.7%
International Hi-Yield Corporate Bond	8.1%	4.5%	0.4%
U.S. Intermediate Government Bond	4.1%	2.5%	0.1%
Cash	10.0%	0.0%	0.0%
TOTAL	100.0%	-	8.4%

Once any position has grown past its target risk limit, the time has come to rebalance the portfolio by shifting some money to other investments currently underweighted based on their risk. For example, selling some small-cap growth, small-cap value, or biotech sector fund shares and using the proceeds to buy more bond or foreign stock fund shares would better balance the maximum potential loss between investments. Thus, the portfolio composition should be readjusted as needed rather than being set just once and left to fate. Portfolio management is dynamic, not static. Last season's top gainers may become victims of their own success. ***Periodic rebalancing to stay diversified is a key tactic to help you buy low, sell high, and limit risk.***

Diversification is not limited to industries and economic sectors. It also applies to company size and Morningstar style. Geographic diversification by different countries in global developed markets (Europe, Australia, Japan, etc.) and emerging markets (China, India, Brazil, South Korea, etc.) can improve investment results as well. The figure below shows that many large, fast growing economies lie outside the United States [Wikipedia, ref 20].

Comparison with economies of individual sovereign countries

Economy	Nominal GDP (billions in USD) - Peak year as of 2019
(01) United States *(Peak in 2019)*	21,439
(02) Eurozone *(Peak in 2008)*	14,188
(03) China *(Peak in 2019)*	14,140
(04) Japan *(Peak in 2012)*	6,203
(05) United Kingdom *(Peak in 2007)*	3,085
(06) India *(Peak in 2019)*	2,936
(07) Brazil *(Peak in 2011)*	2,614
(08) Russia *(Peak in 2013)*	2,289
(09) Canada *(Peak in 2013)*	1,847
(10) Korea *(Peak in 2018)*	1,720
(11) Australia *(Peak in 2012)*	1,569
(12) Mexico *(Peak in 2014)*	1,315

Comparison of the eurozone with other economies

	Population (billions) (2019)	GDP PPP (trillions USD) (2019)	Proportion of world GDP at PPP
Eurozone	0.34	15	10%
European Union	0.45	20	14%
United States	0.33	21	15%
China	1.43	27	19%
India	1.35	11	8%
Japan	0.13	6	4%

The largest economies in the world including Eurozone as a single entity, by Nominal GDP (2019) at their peak level of GDP in billions US$.

The values for EU members that are not also eurozone members are listed both separately and as part of the EU.

Constructive diversification means reducing risk but not diluting winning investments with chronic losers. Your ultimate challenge is to decide which asset classes to include and how much you allocate each to stocks, bonds, cash, real estate, and other assets. Then select and manage specific investments from each asset class. Your asset allocation strategy will rule your long-term investment success; individual stock selection and market-timing are far less crucial tactics. Any investment can be dangerous when it is the only one you have. The Callan Periodic Table of Investment Returns was created in 1999 to show the merits of diversification [Kloepfer, ref 21].

Callan Periodic Table of Investment Returns
Annual Returns for Key Indices Ranked in Order of Performance

2007	2008	2009	2010	2011	2012	2013	2014	2015	2016	2017	2018
Emerging Market Equity 39.38%	U.S. Fixed Income 5.24%	Emerging Market Equity 78.51%	Small Cap Equity 26.85%	U.S. Fixed Income 7.84%	Real Estate 27.73%	Small Cap Equity 38.82%	Real Estate 15.02%	Large Cap Equity 1.38%	Small Cap Equity 21.31%	Emerging Market Equity 37.28%	Cash Equivalent 1.87%
Non-U.S. Equity 12.44%	Non-U.S. Fixed Income 4.39%	High Yield 58.21%	Real Estate 19.63%	High Yield 4.98%	Emerging Market Equity 18.23%	Large Cap Equity 32.39%	Large Cap Equity 13.69%	U.S. Fixed Income 0.55%	High Yield 17.13%	Non-U.S. Equity 24.21%	U.S. Fixed Income 0.01%
Non-U.S. Fixed Income 11.03%	Cash Equivalent 2.06%	Real Estate 37.13%	Emerging Market Equity 18.88%	Non-U.S. Fixed Income 4.36%	Non-U.S. Equity 16.41%	Non-U.S. Equity 21.02%	U.S. Fixed Income 5.97%	Cash Equivalent 0.05%	Large Cap Equity 11.96%	Large Cap Equity 21.83%	High Yield -2.08%
U.S. Fixed Income 6.97%	High Yield -26.16%	Non-U.S. Equity 33.67%	High Yield 15.12%	Large Cap Equity 2.11%	Small Cap Equity 16.35%	High Yield 7.44%	Small Cap Equity 4.89%	Real Estate -0.79%	Emerging Market Equity 11.19%	Small Cap Equity 14.65%	Non-U.S. Fixed Income -2.15%
Large Cap Equity 5.49%	Small Cap Equity -33.79%	Small Cap Equity 27.17%	Large Cap Equity 15.06%	Cash Equivalent 0.10%	Large Cap Equity 16.00%	Real Estate 3.67%	High Yield 2.45%	Non-U.S. Equity -3.04%	Real Estate 4.06%	Non-U.S. Fixed Income 10.51%	Large Cap Equity -4.38%
Cash Equivalent 5.00%	Large Cap Equity -37.00%	Large Cap Equity 26.47%	Non-U.S. Equity 8.95%	Small Cap Equity -4.18%	High Yield 15.81%	Cash Equivalent 0.07%	Cash Equivalent 0.03%	Small Cap Equity -4.41%	Non-U.S. Equity 2.75%	Real Estate 10.36%	Real Estate -5.63%
High Yield 1.87%	Non-U.S. Equity -43.56%	Non-U.S. Fixed Income 7.53%	U.S. Fixed Income 6.54%	Real Estate -6.46%	U.S. Fixed Income 4.21%	U.S. Fixed Income -2.02%	Emerging Market Equity -2.19%	High Yield -4.47%	U.S. Fixed Income 2.65%	High Yield 7.50%	Small Cap Equity -11.01%
Small Cap Equity -1.57%	Real Estate -48.21%	U.S. Fixed Income 5.93%	Non-U.S. Fixed Income 4.95%	Non-U.S. Equity -12.21%	Non-U.S. Fixed Income 4.09%	Emerging Market Equity -2.60%	Non-U.S. Fixed Income -3.09%	Non-U.S. Fixed Income -6.02%	Non-U.S. Fixed Income 1.49%	U.S. Fixed Income 3.54%	Non-U.S. Equity -14.09%
Real Estate -7.39%	Emerging Market Equity -53.33%	Cash Equivalent 0.21%	Cash Equivalent 0.13%	Emerging Market Equity -18.42%	Cash Equivalent 0.11%	Non-U.S. Fixed Income -3.08%	Non-U.S. Equity -4.32%	Emerging Market Equity -14.92%	Cash Equivalent 0.33%	Cash Equivalent 0.86%	Emerging Market Equity -14.58%

Within each asset class, look for investments that consistently offer the highest return with the least risk. The Sharpe (reward to variability) ratio is an investment's historical risk-adjusted return divided by its standard deviation. This ratio measures how well an investment has performed versus its inherent risk. Typically, the risk-adjusted investment return is relative to the 3-month U.S. Treasury bill yield, which is risk-free. The Sharpe ratio is one statistic in the Morningstar risk/return analysis for stock and bond funds. Higher Sharpe ratios indicate better investments that build more wealth and/or offer greater certainty, i.e. peace of mind.

Sharpe ratio = (Average Investment return - Treasury bill yield) / Standard deviation

The Vanguard S&P 500 ETF (VOO) posted a 13.5% average annual total return with a 13.6% standard deviation from 2011 through 2020. Since the three-month US Treasury bill yield averaged 0.6%, the Sharpe ratio was 0.96 for VOO. For all funds in the US large blend category, 0.84 was the average Sharpe ratio.

The red curve in the figure below shows the normal distribution of VOO investment returns from 2011 through 2020. The average dictates the center and the standard deviation determines the spread. Since the high-yield corporate bond fund, PHB, has a much lower standard deviation and average return, the purple curve is sharper and shifted left of VOO. The orange dotted curve represents a perfectly correlated 50/50 mix of VOO and PHB; they move together in the same direction. The combined average return and standard deviation of this pair lie halfway between VOO and PHB. The green dotted curve represents an uncorrelated 50/50 mix of VOO and PHB; they move independently. The combined average return still lies halfway between VOO and PHB, but the standard deviation is reduced [Wikipedia, ref 22]. Hence, the uncorrelated investment portfolio has a greater Sharpe ratio. This synergy defines effective diversification. (VOO and PHB are actually partially correlated.)

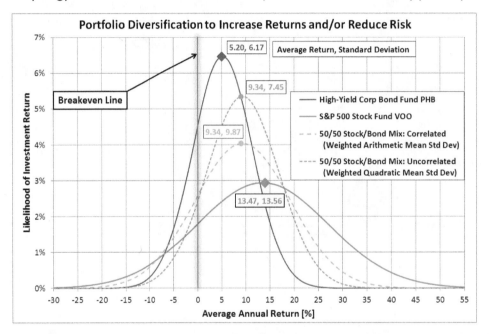

Regardless of your asset allocation, remember that invested assets are always at risk. ***The larger the portfolio and the less time available to recover, the more important it is to protect investments against potential losses.*** Your money management stop-loss points need to be updated as your investments grow.

The original stop-loss point set when each investment position was established protects initially against excessive losses. But, once an investment has progressed significantly, its leash has grown too long. Now it is time to ratchet the stop loss price higher. A trailing stop sell order uses a moving trigger to reset the tolerable loss relative to the recent high instead of the original purchase price. Mountaineers climbing up to the summit set anchors along the way for the same reason, namely to limit the extent of a subsequent fall.

Every investor understandably hesitates to sacrifice the goose that laid the golden egg. However, nothing demonstrates the need for money and risk management better than watching your own wealth vanish while holding positive expected value investments. Set and honor your stop loss points and periodically rebalance assets or brace for a Skinner box penalty beyond your pain limit. Warren Buffet learned two rules of investing from Ben Graham. The first rule is: ***Don't lose money***. The second rule is: ***Don't forget rule number one***.

CHAPTER 6

6) TRACKING GAINS & LOSSES: Quantify and Visualize Growth

Investment success hinges on knowing the score.   Suppose you invest $100 and gain 50% in one year. If you lose 50% the next year, then how much would you have? The answer to this question is really not so simple. Since 50 percent means 50 divided by 100, and the original investment is $100, the first year gain is $50 (0.5 x $100) and your balance is then $150. Likewise, the second year loss is $75 (0.5 x $150) and your balance is then $75. So, you would not break even after 2 years. Instead, your total loss would be $25 or 25% of your original $100 investment. If you lost 50% the first year and then gained 50% the second year, the final result is still a 25% loss overall. Regardless of the order, a 50% incremental gain does not fully offset a 50% incremental loss.

Gain to Reverse Loss	
Loss	Gain
5%	5%
10%	11%
15%	18%
20%	25%
25%	33%
30%	43%
40%	67%
50%	100%

A 50% loss is serious because it takes a 100% gain to recoup your original investment. If you lost 50% the first year, your balance then is $50. A second year gain of 100% equals $50, so your balance is back up to $100. Notice that each year's percentage gain or loss is based on that year's starting balance. So, the 50% loss does not equal the 50% gain because they are based on different balances at different times. Although a 20% loss is not as bad, it still takes a 25% gain to break even again. The adjacent table shows that the loss has to be less than 10% before it offsets the commensurate breakeven gain. This may be confusing because the math of growth and decay is based on multiplication and division instead of addition and subtraction.

When something changes, it appears to be different. The absolute change between one value, V, and a second value considered for reference, Vr, is their arithmetic difference. Vr is typically the value at an earlier time.

$$\text{Absolute change} = V - Vr$$

The relative change is better when discordant types, sizes, or dimensions of things hinder their comparison.

$$\text{Relative change} = (V - Vr) / Vr$$

The relative percentage change, listed in the Gain to Reverse Loss table, is simply 100 times the relative change.

$$\text{Relative percentage change} = 100 * (V - Vr) / Vr$$

The relative percentage change is not symmetric or additive. These flaws cause confusion. Symmetric means that when the two values are reversed, the change is simply inverted. In other words, reversed changes exactly offset each other. Additive means that the combination of incremental changes equals the total overall change. *The way to end this confusion is by using the ratio between V and Vr to quantify growth.* [Tornqvist, ref 23]

$$\text{Growth ratio} = V/Vr$$

The growth ratio is symmetric and additive because multiplication is used to combine changes. Consequently, using the growth ratio (geometric investment return) is always correct. Converting the relative percentage change to its growth ratio is straightforward.

$$\text{Growth ratio} = 1 + (\text{Relative percentage change}/100)$$

For example, if you lost 50% the first year, your balance becomes $50 or 1/2 the original investment. A second year gain of 100% means that the $50 balance doubled to become 2 times its starting value. Multiply the 1/2 ratio from year one times the 2 ratio from year two; the result is 1, the overall growth ratio over both years. The value 1 means the balance now equals the original investment.

Consider the original investment as 100%, i.e. 100/100 = 1. A 50% first year gain means your balance is now 150% or 1.5 times the original value. A 50% second year loss means the balance is 0.5 times the second year starting value. So, the second year balance is 1.5 x 0.5 = 0.75 or 75% of the original investment. This figure means a total loss of 25% over two years.

To recap, always quantify growth using number *ratios* instead of *differences*. Multiply the growth ratio for each period to correctly figure the current balance. ***Use the relative percentage gains and losses only to determine the investment growth ratios.*** Adding relative percentage changes is inherently flawed.

Both relative percentage gains and growth ratios are readily calculated from prices. For example, if the price is $32 initially and then later stands at $40, the growth ratio is $40/$32 = 1.25 or 125% *times* the initial price. The relative percentage gain is 1.25 - 1 = 0.25 or a 25% *more than* the initial price. If the price is $40 initially and then later stands at $32, the growth ratio is $32/$40 = 0.80 or 80% *times* the initial price. The relative percentage loss is 0.80 - 1 = -0.20 or 20% *less than* the initial price. If the price is $32 initially and then later stands at $32, the growth ratio is $32/$32 = 1.00 or 100% *times* the initial price. The relative percentage gain is 1.00 - 1 = 0.00 or a 0% *difference from* the initial price.

If a series of numbers is consistent and simple enough, it is easy to recognize a repeating growth pattern. For example, each data series below can be explained individually and also compared clearly to the others.

Year	1	2	3	4	5	
Data1	1	2	4	8	16	1) Data Series 1 doubles each year
Data2	1	3	9	27	81	2) Data Series 2 triples each year
Data3	10	20	40	80	160	3) Data Series 3 is 10 times Data series 1

These relationships all can be discerned instantly when the data is plotted on the appropriate chart. The first chart uses an arithmetic scale that sets the vertical position of each point. Each full step on this arithmetic scale represents a *difference* of 10. Although consistent growth of each series is clear, it appears that growth is accelerating because each series curves up. It is also not obvious exactly what the growth rate is or how each series truly compares to the other two.

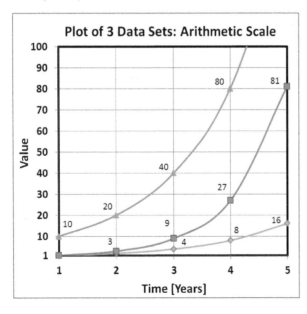
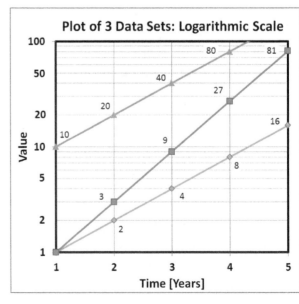

The second chart uses a logarithmic scale that sets the vertical position of each point. Consistent growth is again clear, but now the growth looks constant because each series is a straight line. The slope of each line indicates the growth rate. Series 1 is a straight line whose slope is 2. Series 2 is a straight line whose slope is 3, so it looks 1.5 times steeper. The Series 3 line is parallel to series 1 because they grow at the same rate. The Series 3 line is one full step above the Series 1 line because each full step on this logarithmic scale represents a *ratio* of 10. So, the vertical distance from 10 up to 100 exactly matches the distance from 10 down to 1. These characteristics make perfect sense because the word "logarithm" translated from Greek literally means "ratio of numbers". ***Logarithmic charts clarify growth trends so effectively that it becomes easier to anticipate the next point to come in a consistent series.***

These same principles explain the relative percentage growth reference lines in the Visual Analysis section of the Stock Selection Guide (see page 28). The 5% annual growth line corresponds to a growth ratio of 1.05 over one year. The 10%, 15%, 20%, 25%, and 30% growth lines correspond to 1.10, 1.15, 1.20, 1.25, and 1.30 growth ratios, respectively. Sales, earnings, or stock prices that run parallel to any reference line have grown at that same rate.

Note that the geometric return (growth ratio) for any investment is its sale price divided by its purchase price; hence, "buy low and sell high".

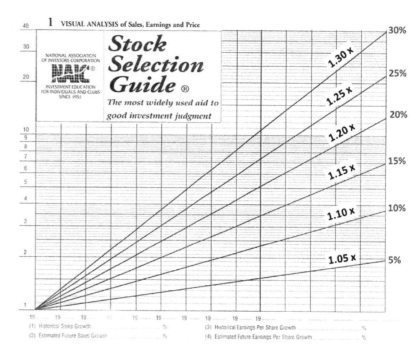

6.1 Price Chart Types – Line Charts, Candlestick Charts, Point & Figure Charts

Regardless of its type, every price chart is a visual summary of an investment's price history. Like a picture that is worth a thousand words, a chart is worth a thousand numbers. Historical prices document investment past performance. They also provide a perspective that helps to forecast future results if the current path continues.

A Line Chart shows how the price of an investment changes over some time period such as a day, a week, a quarter, a year, or even longer. The price at each point is connected to the previous one by a line segment. When many points are included, the chart appears to be a continuous curve. However, when relatively few points are included, the chart looks fragmented. This is like zooming in to view a detailed impressionist painting actually composed of many tiny dots revealed up close.

For example, the next page displays one week's worth of prices plotted once per minute (390 points/day) on the first chart. The prices plotted just once per hour (7 points/day) on the second chart show much less detail. However, the second chart still documents how the price changed sufficiently well for most investors. In any case, it is vital to note the underlying data frequency used in any investment price chart. (Price charts are free from online brokers and at financial websites such as StockCharts and Yahoo Finance.)

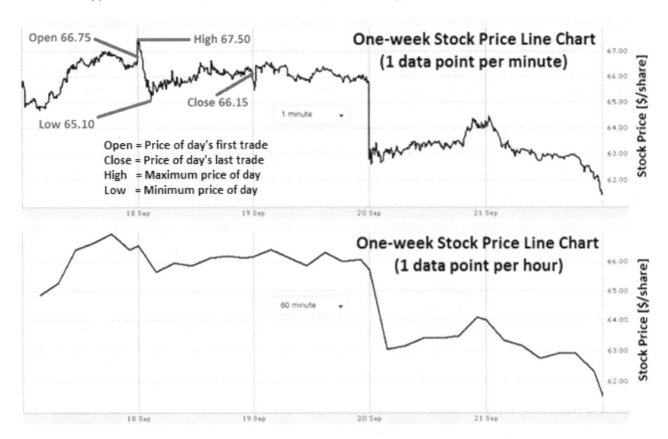

A **Candlestick Chart** displays the four most important prices, namely the high, the low, the open, and the close, as a candlestick to summarize each trading session, typically a day. The candlestick body height shows the price spread, i.e. the difference between the open and the close. ***The body is filled if the close was lower than the open. The body is hollow if the close was higher than the open.*** A wick on top of the body marks a high price greater than both the open and the close. A tail on the bottom of the body marks a low price less than both the open and the close. Compare the same week's prices plotted on the candlestick chart below to the line charts above. Notice how a candlestick shows only the vertical part of a sloping price sequence.

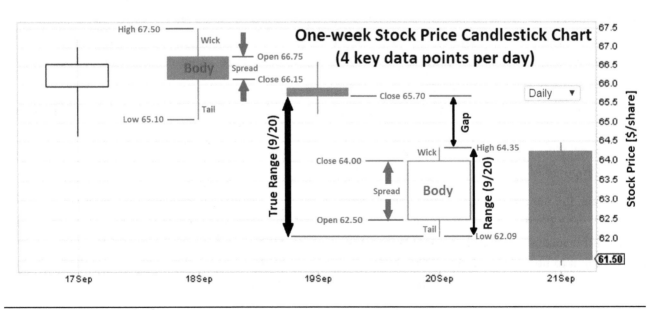

Each candlestick shows the relation between the day's first trade price, the last trade price, the maximum price, and the minimum price. A tall candlestick body indicates strong market sentiment. Investors were optimistic or bullish if the close was above the open, but pessimistic or bearish if the close was below the open. A short candlestick body means weak sentiment. A tail indicates a positive reversal in sentiment, but a wick means a negative mood swing during the trading session. A short candlestick body with a tall wick and a long tail shows indecision. ***A price candlestick is the trading session price history executive summary.***

The true significance of any single candlestick ultimately depends on its position within a broader picture. A sequence of candlesticks may reinforce positive, neutral, or negative market sentiments over many sessions. ***A red candlestick means the close was lower than the prior session close. A black candlestick means that the close was higher than the prior session close.*** So, candlesticks are black when the close is up but red when the close is down. A pattern of lows may depict a price support floor; a pattern of highs may portray a price resistance ceiling.

For example, compared to the daily closing price line chart below, the daily price candlestick chart clarifies significant moves over three months in a single glance. Changing candlestick colors show each closing price reversal between sessions. A switch from red to black denotes a reversal up, but a switch from black to red denotes a reversal down. An unbroken string of candlesticks the same color marks a clear trend up or down.

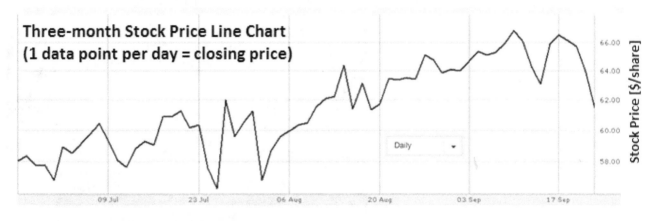

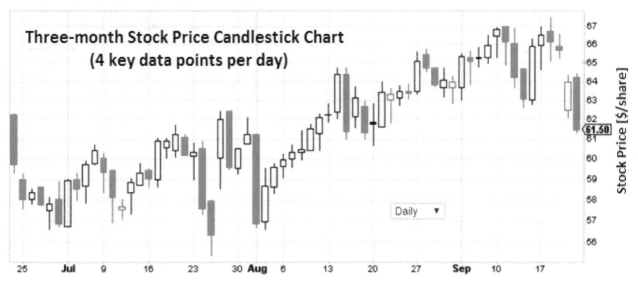

The Point and Figure (P&F) Chart was originally devised to record price movements by hand using X and O symbols marked on graph paper. [Dorsey, ref 24] Each box denotes a price increment, typically a 1% change. An X represents demand causing a 1-box price increase; an O represents supply causing a 1-box price decrease. The X's and O's are sequentially logged in separate columns that alternate to track the price momentum trend. Within any column, the X's only move up and O's only move down.

A price change less than 1 box up or down is ignored; no mark is logged that session. A 1-box price change or more is always marked if it continues the current trend up or down, extending the current column. However, a price change against the current trend must be more significant to signal a legitimate reversal. A 3-box reversal threshold is typically used to determine when a new column is added to the right and acknowledge that price momentum has shifted.

A tall column shows strong sentiment. A column of X's indicates demand is in control; a column of O's indicates supply is in control. *A P&F chart buy signal occurs when the highest price in the current X-column exceeds the high of the previous X-column.* Similarly, a current O-column low below the previous O-column low establishes a P&F sell signal. In short, *each P&F chart column is the executive summary for each price run between reversals instead of just for a single trading session.*

Compared to the previous line and candlestick charts, the P&F chart below distills the same three months of prices into a more concise display. Note how a column shows only the vertical part of a candlestick series.

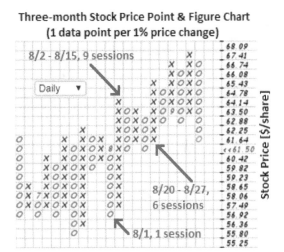

Unbalanced Forces Create Price Movements

A P&F chart typically uses daily closing prices, but the high and low prices can be used instead. The P&F box size and reversal threshold filter out trivial price movements with no time lag. *Although the P&F chart y-axis shows price, the x-axis explicitly shows the number of trend reversals instead of time.* Time is indicated only indirectly as the numbers 1 to 9 or letters A to C that replace the X or O for the 1st price move of each month (Jan = 1, Dec = C). Thus, a P&F chart is designed to reveal the underlying price trends driven by supply and demand, i.e. every pull in the dynamic tug of war between sellers and buyers.

The individual points that comprise a line chart are like single letters of the alphabet. Price candlesticks are like words. Point and Figure chart columns are like sentences. Follow the sequence of letters, words, or sentences long enough, and this information eventually tells a story. Compare the charts below to see which format best conveys the price history for each time period. Weekly data includes one-fifth the points of daily data.

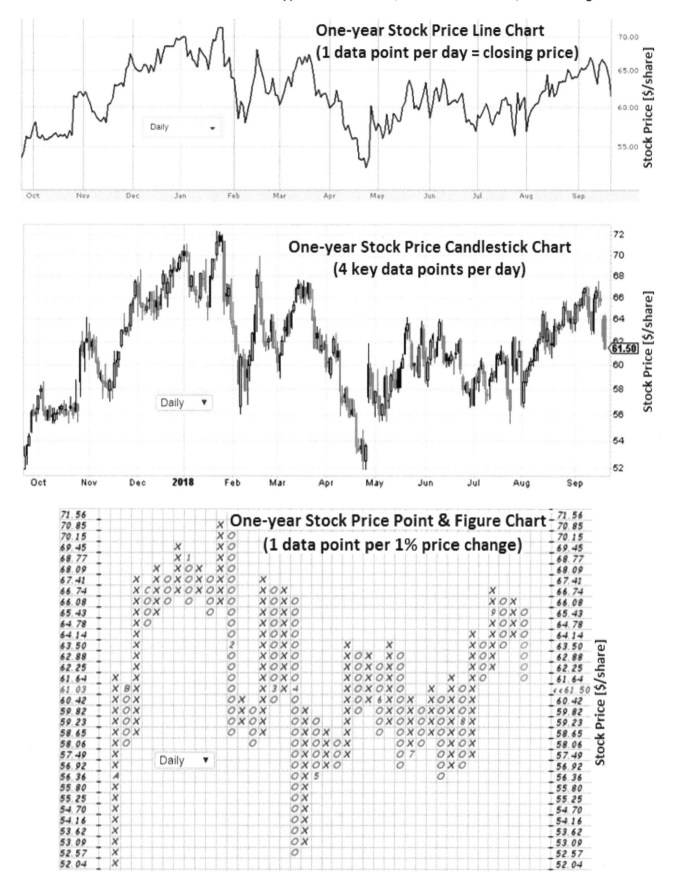

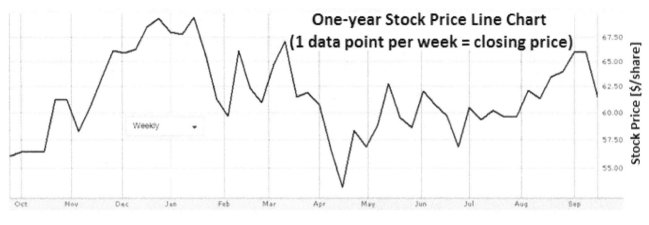

One-year Stock Price Line Chart
(1 data point per week = closing price)

One-year Stock Price Candlestick Chart
(4 key data points per week)

One-year Stock Price Point & Figure Chart
(1 data point per 1% price change)

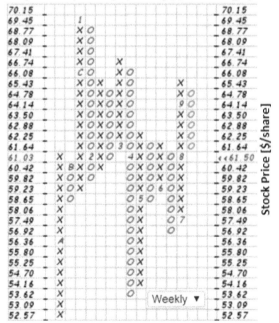

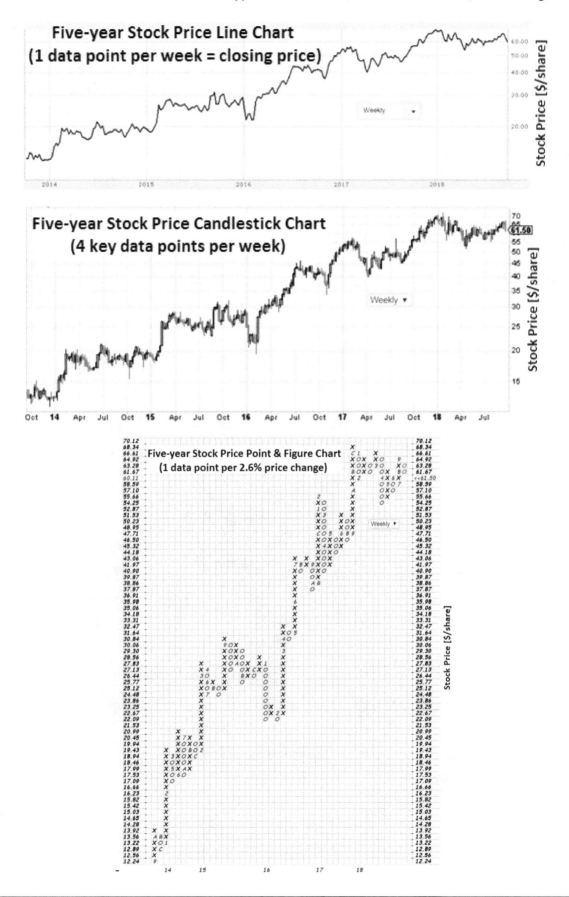

Five-year Stock Price Line Chart
(1 data point per week = closing price)

Five-year Stock Price Candlestick Chart
(4 key data points per week)

Five-year Stock Price Point & Figure Chart
(1 data point per 2.6% price change)

The different five-year charts all tell the same story of consistent long-term growth despite some short-term zigzags. This trajectory is typical for a fundamentally sound long-term investment. A brief price history recap puts all the previous price charts into proper perspective. The most current week showed a clear trend down as the price dropped by almost 10% (decay). However, the most current quarter showed a clear trend up where the high price peaked 20% above the low price (growth). The overall trend for the past year was flat (equilibrium) but volatile with price swings up and down spanning 35% of the year's median price. Over the last five years, the price grew from 12 to 70, almost 6 times its initial value (growth). Hence, if the fundamental business success story remains intact, the latest price could be a reasonable long-term buying opportunity despite the bumpy ride.

In any case, check long, medium, & short-term time frames using five-year, two-year, one-year, six-month, and three-month charts to put the current price into historical context. Each chart contributes part of the story to the next longer one and shows how the price history evolved to reach today's position. These charts fit together like traditional nesting dolls. The longest chart contains the most information just like the largest doll contains the most descendants inside. Trace the full lineage back to make sure you understand the whole story. Nested time frame comparisons can help spot when a short-term loss may be part of a long-term gain.

6.2 Stock Market Price Fluctuations

Legendary investor Warren Buffet was mentored by Ben Graham, the "dean of security analysis" and "father of value investing". Consider Graham's perspective on price fluctuations for reference as shown below:

"Imagine you own a small share of a private business. One of your partners, named Mr. Market, is uniquely obliging. Each day, he tells you what he thinks your share is worth and offers either to buy it from you or sell you more on that basis. Sometimes his value seems credible and justified by your understanding of business developments and prospects. But, his value often seems silly when enthusiasm or fear overwhelms him.

Will you let Mr. Market's daily message dictate the value of your share? If you are a sensible businessman or prudent investor, you only will if you agree with him or *if you want to trade with him*. You may be happy to sell out to him when he quotes an absurdly high price, and equally happy to buy from him when his price is ridiculously low. Otherwise, you will be wiser to establish your own estimate of how much your share is worth. This very situation arises whenever an investor owns a listed common stock." [Graham, ref 25]

To reach a deal, a buyer and seller ironically must disagree. The buyer must prefer the merchandise instead of his money, but the seller must prefer the money instead of his merchandise. This disagreement is resolved when they strike a deal. No difference of opinion means no deal. When the buyer and seller both agree that the merchandise is more valuable, the buyer's bid price is too low for the seller. When the buyer and seller both agree that the money is more valuable, the seller's ask price is too high for the buyer.

Your aim as an investor is to find and capitalize on opportunities disguised as such disagreements. Price fluctuations are significant because they offer opportunities to buy wisely when prices fall sharply and to sell wisely after prices advance a great deal. To effectively apply this buy low and sell high strategy, it helps to consider any stock price range in terms of price zones as shown below.

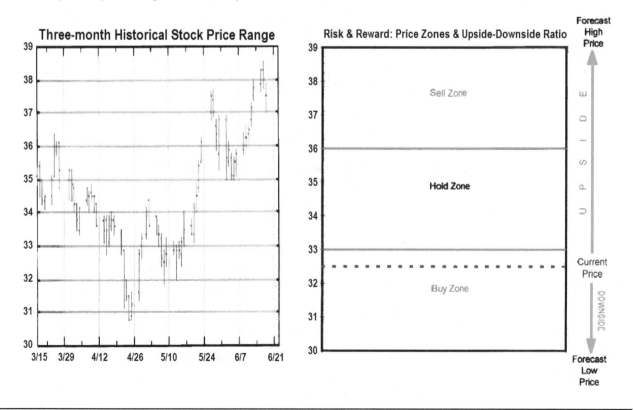

The ideal time to buy this stock was when the share price dipped below $31 just before April 26th. The ideal time to sell this stock was when the price peaked above $38 around June 14th. The right time to hold was when the price was halfway between these two extremes. Since an investor has three possible responses to the daily market price, dividing the price range into three distinct zones creates price targets to trigger action. For three equal zones, prices below $33 would be reasonable buying opportunities and prices above $36 would be reasonable selling junctures. Prices between $33 and $36 would prompt no action. This strategy becomes clear to execute when the price zones are superimposed onto the price history below.

Notice that at the $33 buying threshold, the maximum loss would have been less than $3 per share since the price stayed above $30. On the other hand, the top gain would have been nearly $6 per share since the price came close to $39. Therefore, this situation presented a $6 upside reward and a $3 downside risk, i.e. an upside/downside ratio of 2:1. *If a bird in the hand is really worth two in the bush, a sensible buyer should view a higher ratio as an incentive to enter the investment Skinner box.*

At the $36 selling threshold, the maximum loss would have been nearly $6 per share since the price dropped close to $30. On the other hand, the top gain would have been less than $3 per share because the price stayed

---

below $39. Thus, this situation presented a $3 upside reward and a $6 downside risk, i.e. an upside/downside ratio of 1:2. ***A prudent seller should regard a lower ratio as motivation to exit the Skinner box.***

A more demanding investor could expand the HOLD zone to 1/2 instead of 1/3 the entire price range. This expansion would compress the BUY zone to 1/4 the entire range and give a 3:1 upside/downside ratio at a $32.25 buying threshold. This expansion would also compress the SELL zone to 1/4 the entire range and give a 1:3 upside/downside ratio at a $36.75 selling threshold. Thus, the wider HOLD zone would ultimately mean better risk/reward odds at the expense of fewer transaction opportunities.

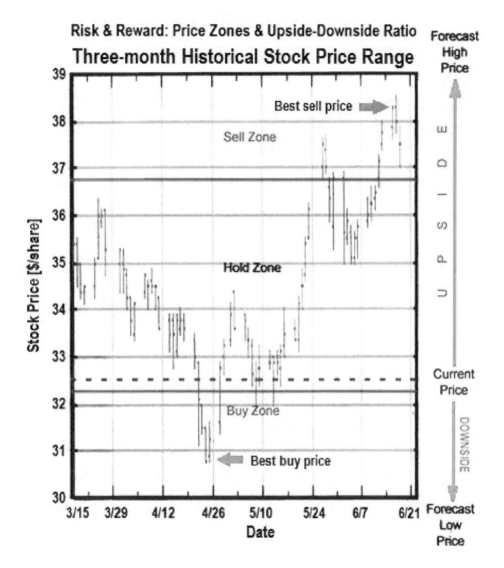

Price zones are perfect in hindsight, but not when predicting the future. It is simple to overlay price zones on a three-month price history to check past results. It is much more challenging to forecast future high and low prices for the next three to five years to establish SSG zones now that provide profitable action guidelines. Section 4 of the Stock Selection Guide details a procedure to figure price zones, downside risk, and upside reward (see p 29). The estimated high price is figured from the past five-year average high P/E times earnings per share forecast five years into the future. The estimated low price can be reckoned by choosing the most suitable method from those listed on the following page.

Stock Selection Guide methods used to estimate a future five-year low price:

        a) The average low P/E times the current or lowest anticipated future earnings

        b) The past five-year average low price

        c) The recent severe market low price

        d) The current dividend divided by the past five-year high dividend yield

        e) The current 52-week high times the five-year average low price / high price ratio

The main purpose of price zones is to estimate a reasonable stock purchase price based on the company's fundamental value. This reflects the Ben Graham and Warren Buffet value tenets. Price zones also forecast a rational sale price to establish when a stock has run too far "out over its skis". These buy and sell prices are not designed to encourage short-term trading, but to serve as value guidelines that are updated quarterly after sales and earnings are reported.

Don't be a perfectionist when you set the buy or sell price on an investment trade. No player hits a tennis ball right on the line every time. Hit the ball out, and you lose. Aim inside the line instead with a margin that still wins.

CHAPTER 7

7)   <u>WHEN TO ACT: Technical Indicators to Sense the Investment Environment</u>

All living organisms are distinguished by their capacity to detect, respond, and adapt to their environment. They behave intentionally, not randomly. In fact, each organism is designed to react to external stimuli based on the sensations perceived. Sharks have sensors that detect electric impulses generated by prey. Pit vipers can sense infrared waves radiated from a warm animal. Flying bats emit ultrasonic sounds and listen to their echoes to determine the distance to objects, their size, texture, and velocity. Honey bees and homing pigeons sense direction from the earth's magnetic field to navigate their way home. Humans have five basic senses, namely sight, hearing, smell, taste, and touch.

If your life depended on your ability to correctly sense fire, you might be alert to signs of smoke first because you believe that where there is smoke, there is fire. If you smell smoke, you realize that something became hot enough to generate vapor. But, some smells, like overheated brakes or an electric power cord short circuit, indicate heat without fire, so your evidence is not yet conclusive. Your probability of detecting fire by smell alone is less than 100%.

Since seeing is believing, you might use your eyes to look for smoke and flames. However, if you have only witnessed the orange flame of burning wood or the blue flame of natural gas combustion, you might not recognize the smokeless, transparent flame of burning methanol as revealed during the 1981 Indianapolis 500 automobile race. You could also be fooled by the display of a modern electric faux fireplace that actually has no fire. So, you might not have fire even if you see flames and you could have fire even when you see no flames. Thus, your chance of correctly sensing fire only by sight is also below 100%.

But you need not rely solely on sight, smell, or any single sense. You naturally link independent sources of evidence together. If you smelled smoke and saw flames, you would be more certain of your judgment. You might be motivated to move if you also felt radiant heat. Your ears would probably recognize the sound of crackling wood. If you smelled the smoke, saw the flames, felt the heat, heard the crackling, and tasted grilled food or roasted marshmallows, you could be pretty darn sure the fire was real. It all adds up. Your five different senses have confirmed the same conclusion. Of course, whenever you sense fire, you still need to decide if you should flee for your life or get closer instead so you don't freeze to death.

An independent signal provides information based on a unique principle not used by other signals. The probability that two random, independent events will occur simultaneously is the probability of the first event happening individually times the probability of the second individual event. For example, the probability that a flipped coin will land heads up is 1/2 or 50%. The probability that rolling a single cube of dice will turn up a six is 1/6 or 16.7%. Since the coin flip result does not affect the dice roll outcome and vice versa, the chance of heads AND a six is 1/2 x 1/6 = 1/12 or 8.3%. The chance that something else will happen is 91.7% by difference because the probability of all outcomes totals 100%.

A perfect signal has a 100% probability of being correct. A random guess about two equally possible outcomes has a 50% chance of being correct. If a specific signal has a 60% probability of being correct, then it also has a **40%** chance of being incorrect. If another independent signal also has a 60% probability of being right, then the probability that both of them are wrong at the same time is just **16%**.

Total probability of failure = (Chance Signal 1 fails) x (Chance Signal 2 fails) = 0.4 x 0.4 = 0.16 or 16%

The probability that three such independent signals are all wrong at the same time drops to **6.4%**.

Total probability of failure = 0.4 x 0.4 x 0.4 = 0.064 or 6.4%

The probability that four such independent signals are all wrong at the same time is **2.6%.**

Total probability of failure = 0.4 x 0.4 x 0.4 x 0.4 = 0.026 or 2.6%

The probability that five such independent signals are all wrong at the same time is **1.0%.**

Total probability of failure = 0.4 x 0.4 x 0.4 x 0.4 x 0.4 = 0.010 or 1.0%

This math shows how much your chance of success improves every time you recognize another independent signal even though each one could be wrong. In this case, one signal means 60% success, two signals mean 84% success, three mean 93.6% success, etc. In this manner, the union of independent events can be leveraged to improve your chances of reward despite the risks posed by the investment environment today. [Appel, ref 26] You insist on positive confirmation from multiple signals before you decide that the time to act is now. If signals conflict, you need not gamble. Play it safe while you sort them out. ***When you incorporate complementary indicators into your buy and sell decisions, you improve your investment Skinner box chances of reward instead of punishment.***

Your need to see, interpret, and respond to signals when you invest is comparable to the training required to earn your license and drive a car. You must first pass a vision exam, written test, and driving test to verify that you can maneuver safely despite the inherent dangers. You move forward when your path is clear, but when it isn't, you wait instead, watch other drivers, and monitor the signals. Cross the railroad tracks at the wrong time, and you create a train wreck. Don't blame it on the train.

TECHNICAL INDICATORS

From a technical view, a stock's price is just the most recent agreement negotiated by buyers and sellers. Technical indicators focus on stock trade statistics regardless of the underlying, intrinsic business value determined from sales, earnings, profit margins, or free cash flow. Since financial markets record the number of shares exchanged and the price paid for every single transaction during each trading session, indicators actually apply to nearly everything that is publicly traded. Regardless of the merchandise exchanged, technical analysis aims to assess what has happened, but doesn't really explain why.

Technical indicators are scorecards. Every indicator analyzes an investment's trade history using a unique numerical recipe to compute results from input data, namely price and/or volume. This recipe is periodically executed to generate a sequence of results often displayed visually as a trajectory or pattern. Both the input data and the calculations used to extract information dictate an indicator's significance. Each class of technical indicators adds an independent investment signal to complement others and help clarify the story.

Most indicators create a distinct signature for each ticker symbol because its price-volume trade history is unique. Hence, technical indicators may apply to a single stock, a sector of stocks, an entire stock market index, bonds, funds, currencies, or commodities like oil, gold, or corn. However, a few different indicators always only apply to a specific collection of investments. In any case, make sure to understand what specific investments your technical indicator refers to. The distinction between an individual, a small group, or an entire population obviously makes a big difference for proper interpretation.

Some technical indicators are compared directly to an investment's price history. They are superimposed on the price chart and use the same vertical scale as prices. This arrangement helps distinguish relatively high and low prices, clarify the price trend, and locate where the price may be bounded by support below or resistance above. Moving averages, Keltner Channels, Bollinger Bands, and Volume by Price are examples of indicators that are displayed as price chart overlays. Specific cases are illustrated later in this chapter.

Other technical indicators stand alone because their value is not directly comparable to price. They share the price history time span on the horizontal scale, but use a different vertical scale than prices. These indicators are stacked above or below the price chart. This layout helps reveal where an indicator either validates the price or contradicts it and consequently implies a price continuation or a forthcoming reversal. Trading session volume, RSI, MACD, PPO, BPI, and VIX are examples of indicators that are displayed separately from price.

Although dozens of technical indicators are readily available online to supplement a basic price chart, more are not necessarily better. A handful of complementary indicators suffice to show whether buyers, sellers, or neither now control the action. ***An investor would do well to check just one single indicator from each of the five following types: trend, momentum, volume, breadth, and sentiment.*** One specific example would include a moving average, RSI, session volume, BPI, and VIX. Other diverse combinations would also lead to the same overall conclusion.

Although any situation depicted by indicators can persist indefinitely, extreme cases sooner or later revert back to the mean, i.e. average state. Periods of little movement often lead to a breakout up or down. A run of big moves often then stabilizes. Prices typically climb up slowly but sometimes drop suddenly in response to new information. Indicators definitely display a wide variety of patterns that evolve continuously.

7.1 Trend Indicators - Moving Averages

A Moving Average provides a centerline on a stock price chart. Sequential prices that move in the same direction establish a trend over time. An upward trend continues as long as the price stays above its average. This incline means progress. A downward trend continues when the price stays below its average. This decline means regression. *The moving average marks the middle of the road to show that your investment vehicle is in the proper lane moving in the right direction instead of veering off course into the wrong lane.*

Stock prices meander like a butterfly that never lands. Consider the price sequence below. A simple moving average (SMA) of the most recent five points gives a smoother trajectory. Each of these 5 points contributes *20%* (1/5) to the average value. The simple moving average value plotted at age 2 is computed below.

SMA5 = **95.6** x *20%* + **94.2** x *20%* + **94.3** x *20%* + **93.3** x *20%* + **92.9** x *20%* = 94.0   **(Prices 4 to 0 included)**

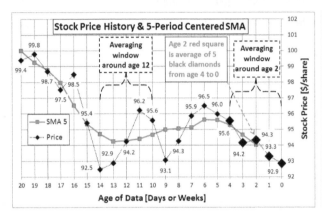
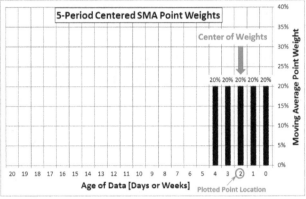

The moving average point series makes it easy to follow the underlying price trend. About half the prices lie above the red trend line; and about half the prices are below the red line. The moving average turning locations generally coincide with price reversals. Notice that the 5-point SMA values centered at ages 1 and 0 are not shown because they require future prices not yet available. Once the next trading session closes, the new price is included into the SMA and the oldest price is dropped as the active 5-point window steps forward.

If the simple moving average uses the trailing 5 points instead of a centered averaging window, the latest average price is plotted at age 0, the current date. *The whole red trend curve shifts 2 time periods to the right.*

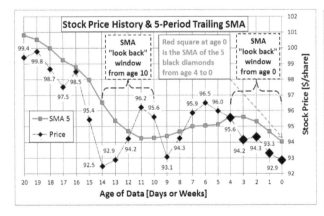
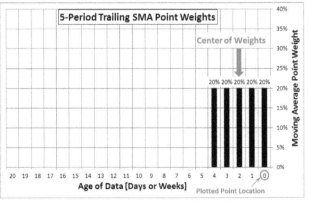

The moving average turns now lag behind price reversals. Consequently, the prices cross the trailing SMA four times versus nine times for the centered SMA. *Each cross down is a wrong turn; each cross up is back on track.*

A simple moving average of the most recent 11 points dampens the trend further. In this case, the average age of the prices included is (11 − 1)/2 = 5 time periods before the most recent date. Each of these 11 points contributes *9.1%* (1/11) to the simple moving average value at age 5 as shown below.

SMA11 = **95.6** x *9.1%* + **93.1** x *9.1%* + **94.3** x *9.1%* + **95.9** x *9.1%* + **96.5** x *9.1%* + **96.0** x *9.1%* ... **(Prices 10 - 5)**

+ **95.6** x *9.1%* + **94.2** x *9.1%* + **94.3** x *9.1%* + **93.3** x *9.1%* + **92.9** x *9.1%* = 94.7   **(Prices 4 - 0)**

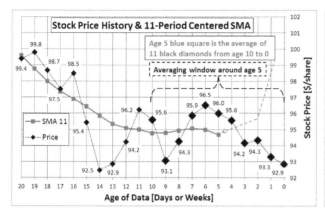

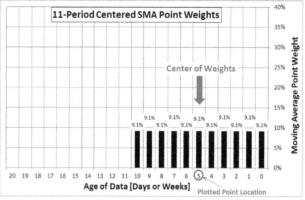

This moving average series shows a less responsive underlying trend. About half the prices still lie above the blue trend line; and about half the prices are below the blue line. But, this 11-point SMA does not clearly show the same two turns as the 5-point SMA. Notice that the 11-point moving average values centered at ages 4, 3, 2, 1, and 0 are not shown because they require future prices not yet available.

If the simple moving average uses the trailing 11 points instead of a centered averaging window, the latest average price is plotted at age 0, the current date. *The entire blue trend curve shifts 5 time periods to the right.*

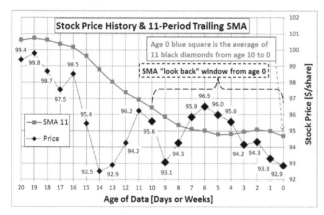

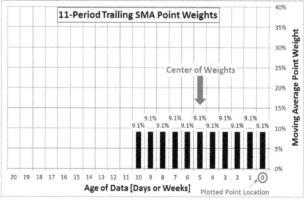

The moving average now lags further behind price movements. The prices cross the trailing SMA line just twice and omits four more crosses left of age 8 shown by the centered SMA.

The 5-point and 11-point SMA examples demonstrate the inherent tradeoff between trailing moving average smoothness and time delay. Filtering out noise clarifies a smooth trend, but also delays recognition of trend reversals when they occur. Effectively following the trend and accurately identifying reversals without false alarms can make investing profitable if the price range and duration are large enough to incite action. *An investor can never be sure to buy before the price goes up, but CAN buy after a price drop occurs. An investor can never be sure to sell before the price goes down, but CAN sell after a price gain occurs.*

A simple moving average weights all points equally. In contrast, an exponential moving average (EMA) weights newer points more than older ones. The weights decay in a geometric progression as the data points age. For example, an EMA that uses the following weight sequence:

0.1% 0.2% 0.3% 0.4% 0.6% 0.9% 1.3% 2.0% 2.9% 4.4% 6.6% 9.9% 14.8% 22.2% 33.3%

has the same average price age as a 5-point SMA. Hence, this moving average is called a 5-point EMA even though the most recent 5 points account for only 87% of the total average value. The most recent 15 points account for almost 100% of the total average value. The size of these points corresponds to their EMA weights in the price plots below. The EMA value at age 0 can be computed from scratch as follows:

EMA5 = **92.5** x *0.1%* + **92.9** x *0.2%* + **94.2** x *0.3%* + **96.2** x *0.4%* + **95.6** x *0.6%* ...   **(Prices 14 - 10)**

+ **93.1** x *0.9%* + **94.3** x *1.3%* + **95.9** x *2.0%* + **96.5** x *2.9%* + **96.0** x *4.4%* ...   **(Prices 9 - 5)**

+ **95.6** x *6.6%* + **94.2** x *9.9%* + **94.3** x *14.8%* + **93.3** x *22.2%* + **92.9** x *33.3%* = 93.7   **(Prices 4 - 0)**

Note that because its weight is tiny, the oldest price included makes only a marginal contribution to an EMA.

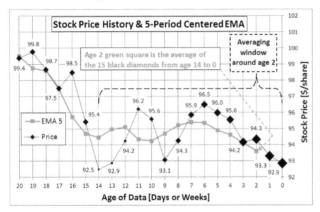

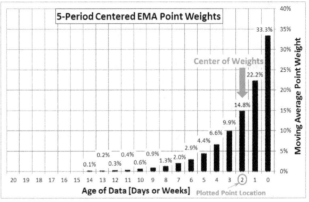

This moving average series shows a more responsive underlying trend. It includes 4 reversals. The prices are still well distributed above and below the green trend line. Notice that the 5-point moving average values centered at ages 1 and 0 are not shown because they require future prices not yet available.

If the exponential moving average uses the trailing points instead of a centered averaging window, the latest average price is plotted at age 0, the current date. **The entire green trend curve shifts right by 2 time periods.**

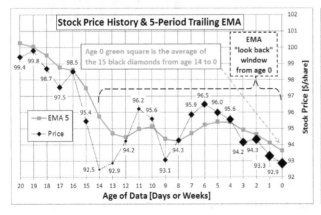

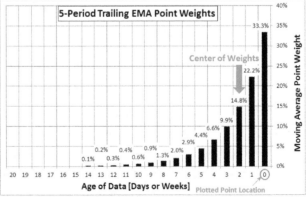

The trailing EMA lags behind price reversals. Prices cross the trailing EMA much like the centered EMA.

Exponential averaging is like the psychology of learning when prior understanding is updated by new experience. Each time step forward, an EMA combines a fraction of new information with all prior information discounted by the same fraction, the "tracking rate". So, an EMA is easy to update from its previous value when a new price is observed. *Since the age 0 EMA weight sets how much new information is included, this 5-point EMA is also called a "33% trend".* A tracking rate of 2/(N+1) gives an EMA the same average price age as an N-point SMA.

New Trend   = **New Information** x *Tracking Rate* + **Previous Trend** x *(1 – Tracking Rate)*

EMA5 @ Age 0   =   **Price @ Age 0**   x   *Weight 0*   + **EMA5 @ Age 1** x *(100% - Weight 0)*

EMA5 @ Age 0   =   **92.9**   x   33.3%   +   **94.1**   x   66.7%   = **93.7**

Moving Average Price Crossovers

A 200-day SMA looks back in time 9 ½ months, i.e. 40 weeks, and is the most common long-term trend indicator. A 50-day SMA looks back 10 weeks and is a popular shorter-term trend indicator. Short-term moving average crossovers are more common and less significant than a long-term moving average crossover. When the price crosses above its 200-day SMA, it is a "bullish" or favorable sign. Conversely, whenever the price crosses below its 200-day SMA, it is a "bearish" or adverse sign.

Moving Average Double Crossovers

A "golden cross" occurs when the 50-day SMA crosses above the 200-day SMA. This is even more bullish than a price cross above the 200-day SMA. During a bullish run, the price typically first crosses above the 50-day SMA, then above the 200-day SMA, and then the 50-day SMA crosses above the 200-day SMA. Investors prize three parallel rising trajectories: the price above the 50-day SMA above the 200-day SMA. The price is simultaneously making short-term progress and long-term progress in this case.

A "death cross" occurs when the 50-day SMA crosses below the 200-day SMA. This is even more bearish than a price cross below the 200-day SMA. During a bearish run, the price typically first crosses below the 50-day SMA, then below the 200-day SMA, and then the 50-day SMA crosses below the 200-day SMA. Investors despise three parallel falling trajectories: the price below the 50-day SMA below the 200-day SMA. The price is now losing ground in both the short-term and long-term. Moving average crossover examples for an S&P 500 stock index ETF are shown on the 2-year chart of daily data below.

Investment charts online today do not display centered moving averages, only trailing moving averages. As shown by the previous examples, trailing averages effectively filter out noise from fluctuating prices but always create a delay in the process. The delay increases when more points are averaged. The weights of the included points affect the trailing average values and the delay. For any trailing average, the noise reduction benefit should be balanced against the cost of recognizing trend movements late.

Compared to the latest price, the trailing average is always late because it includes old prices from previous times. When prices continually increase, a trailing moving average is always below the actual price because all the old prices are lower prices. When prices continually decrease, a trailing average is always above the actual price because all the old prices are higher prices. In any case, the momentum has already reversed once the price crosses the trailing moving average regardless of its type and how many points it includes.

Moving averages indicate trends outright, but they also serve as building blocks incorporated into other technical indicators such as MACD, PPO, PVO, Bollinger Bands, Keltner Channels, and McClellan oscillators. Haurlan [ref 27] describes how moving averages were originally used to keep guided missiles on target.

7.2 Momentum Indicators - RSI, MACD, PPO

Momentum is the quantity of motion possessed by a moving object and tends to keep it moving. The momentum of a train depends directly on both the distance it travels each second and how many railcars are connected together. A ball rolling downhill has momentum, as does a helium balloon going up. The balloon and ball tethered in perfect balance have no momentum because the opposing forces are equal. Figuratively, momentum means the tendency of something to repeat a recent trend. Investment momentum refers to a sequence of prices that continues to move in the same direction, either up or down.

The Relative Strength Index (RSI) quantifies the average gain versus the average loss based on closing prices for a single investment over a specific number of time periods, typically the previous 14 trading days. This time span is almost three weeks since the U.S. stock market is closed on weekends and holidays. Trading occurs on the remaining 252 days per year, i.e. 21 days each month. The term "relative strength" generally refers to the performance ratio of two different investments, but RSI always denotes single asset price momentum.

A higher price means demand was stronger when the trading session closed. Tally the price gains from the last 14 sessions. Divide this tally by 14 to quantify the average gain when demand was strong. A lower closing price shows weaker demand. Sum the price losses and divide by 14 to quantify the average loss when demand was weak. The average gain divided by the average loss, i.e. relative strength, provides a ratio that quantifies how strong the overall demand was during that time period. The relative strength index scales this ratio from 0 for no demand to 100 for infinite demand.

When the average daily gain is equal to the average loss, the RSI is 50. The price has taken one step up for every step down, i.e. no net price change. The price simply moved sideways. When the gain to loss ratio is 3/7, the RSI is 30. The price has taken just 3 steps up for every 7 steps down. The investment is now considered to be oversold, i.e. a clearance sale. An RSI equal to 0 means the price has decayed incessantly for 14 straight sessions without taking even one step up. This case is free fall. When the gain to loss ratio is 7/3, the RSI is 70. The price has taken 7 steps up for every 3 steps down. The investment is now considered to be overbought, i.e. a bidding war. An RSI equal to 100 means the price has grown continually for 14 consecutive sessions without taking even one step down. This case is lift-off.

The RSI value for age 0 is computed below from scratch for the same price sequence previously considered.

AGE	14	13	12	11	10	9	8	7	6	5	4	3	2	1	0
PRICE	92.5	92.9	94.2	96.2	95.6	93.1	94.3	95.9	96.5	96.0	95.6	94.2	94.3	93.3	92.8
CHANGE	↑0.4	↑1.4	↑2.0	↓(0.6)	↓(2.5)	↑1.2	↑1.6	↑0.6	↓(0.5)	↓(0.4)	↓(1.4)	↑0.2	↓(1.0)	↓(0.5)

Total gains ↑ = 0.4 + 1.4 + 2.0 + 1.2 + 1.6 + 0.6 + 0.2 = 7.3   Average gain = 7.3 / 14 = 0.52

Total losses ↓ = (0.6) + (2.5) + (0.5) + (0.4) + (1.4) + (1.0) + (0.5) = (7.0)   Average loss = (7.0) / 14 = (0.50)

Relative Strength: RS = Average Gain / Average Loss = 0.52 / (0.50) = 1.05

Relative Strength Index: RSI = 100 − 100 / [1 + RS] = 100 − 100 / [1 + 1.05] = 51.3

To reduce RSI fluctuations, exponential averaging is applied to calculate the 14-day average gains and losses before the RS ratio is figured. The tracking rate used is 1/14. The smoothed RSI is plotted below in purple.

New 14-day Exponential Average = **New Price Change** x *1/14* + **Previous 14-day Average** x *13/14*

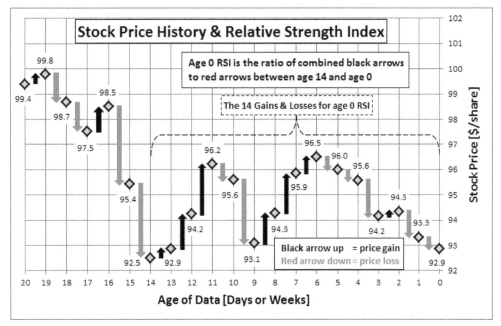

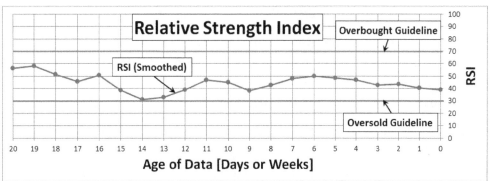

The proper action to take during a clearance sale or bidding war ultimately depends on the true value you assess for the merchandise being traded. However, *the RSI oversold & overbought guidelines of 30 & 70 are rumble strips that give warning before an investment vehicle goes off the road on the low side or high side.*

The Moving Average Convergence/Divergence (MACD) tracks the difference between two average prices. A 12-day EMA (EMA12) of closing prices is typically compared to a 26-day EMA (EMA26). Since the 26-day EMA includes more prices that extend further back in time, it estimates an older average price that changes gradually. The 12-day EMA includes fewer prices, so it estimates a newer, more sensitive average price. When price loses momentum, these moving averages converge. When price gains momentum, these averages diverge. So, **this coupled short and long EMA pair is used to derive price velocity and acceleration to pinpoint price reversals**.

The chart below shows a 40-day price history (blue) along with its 12-day (pink) and 26-day (black) *centered* exponential moving averages. The 12-day centered EMA price is 94.70 at age 5½. EMA12 values to the right are not shown because they require future prices not yet available. Likewise, the 26-day centered EMA price is 95.65 at age 12½. EMA26 values to the right also require future prices not yet available. A green dotted line connects these EMA12 and EMA26 points because each one includes the same most recent price from age 0.

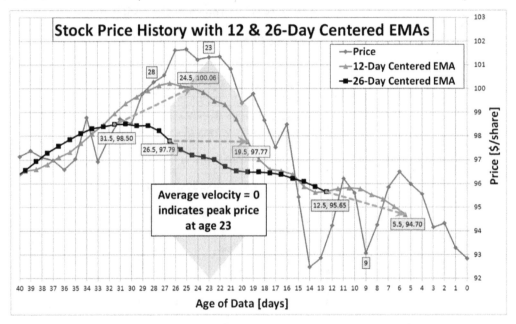

The weighted average age of prices included in the 26-day EMA is 12½ days before the current closing price. The average age of prices in the 12-day EMA is 5½ days before the latest closing price. So each 26-day EMA price has a data window centered 7 days before the corresponding 12-day EMA price. Hence, every pair of matching EMA12 and EMA26 points depicts two different average prices at two different times 7 days apart.

The average rate of change between 2 points is their difference in position over time, i.e. the velocity. The green dotted line slopes down between EMA12 point [5.5, 94.70] and EMA26 point [12.5, 95.65]. The price difference was 94.70 − 95.65 = -0.95 between age 5.5 and age 12.5. Since age 9 lies halfway in between, the average price velocity was -0.95 at age 9, i.e. 9 days ago. The price was then falling.

Looking back from age 14, the average age of prices included in the 12-day centered EMA is 5½ days earlier. The 26-day centered EMA price age is 12½ days earlier. The green dotted line is *horizontal* between EMA12 point [19.5, 97.77] and EMA26 point [26.5, 97.79]. The price difference was 97.77 − 97.79 = -0.02 between age 19.5 and age 26.5. So at the age 23 midway point, the average price velocity was -0.02. *The price had then peaked.*

Looking back from age 19, the 12-day and 26-day centered EMA price ages are respectively 5½ days and 12½ days earlier. The green dotted line slopes up between the points EMA12 [24.5, 100.06] and EMA26 [31.5, 98.50].

The price difference was 100.06 − 98.50 = +1.56 between age 24.5 and age 31.5. So, the average price velocity was +1.56 at the age 28 midway point. The price was then rising.

If the 12-day EMA uses trailing points instead of a centered averaging window, the latest average price is plotted at age 0, the current date. The pink EMA12 curve shifts right 5½ days on the chart below. If the 26-day EMA uses trailing points, the black EMA26 curve shifts right 12½ days. The 7-day offset between the EMA12 and EMA26 curves is eliminated. They now cross at age 14. A cross means that the price velocity is 0, but this was actually true 9 days earlier at age 23. This 9-day lag is the median delay from the two trailing EMAs.

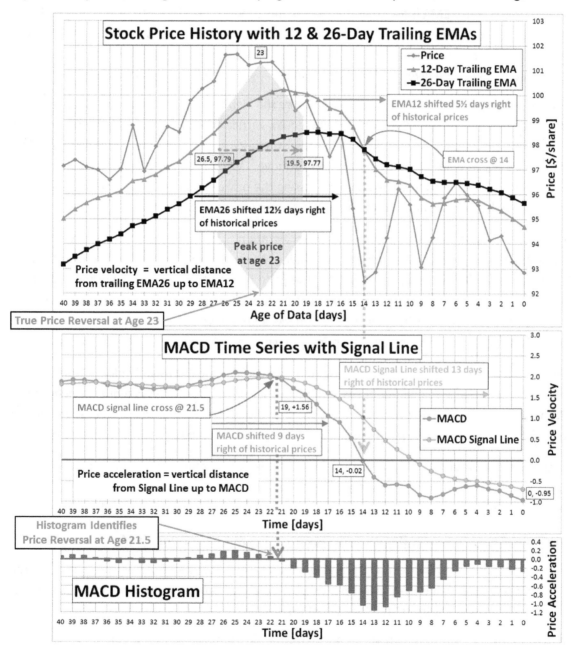

The 12-day trailing EMA minus the 26-day trailing EMA is called the MACD time series. The MACD chart above includes the same three velocities previously depicted by the EMA green dotted lines. The time versus velocity coordinates [19,+1.56], [14,-0.02], and [0,-0.95] express the price velocities delayed by 9 days (teal curve above).

The MACD time series is a speedometer that quantifies how fast the price is moving, either up or down. MACD indicates the price curve slope at any point, i.e., the price velocity. When the price increases, its velocity is positive, and the MACD series is above zero. When the price decreases, its velocity is negative, and the MACD series is below zero. When the price stops, its velocity is zero, and the MACD series is at zero. MACD readings are significant because the price always stops before it reverses direction up or down.

A moving average of the MACD time series itself creates a reference velocity. This baseline is called the MACD signal line (orange) and is typically a 9-day trailing EMA of the MACD series. The weighted average age of all velocities included in this 9-day EMA is four days before the most recent velocity. Hence, every pair of matching MACD and EMA9 signal line points depicts two different average velocities at two different times four days apart. When price velocity decreases, the MACD series and its signal line converge. When price velocity increases, MACD and its signal line diverge. See the teal and orange curves on the previous page, middle chart.

The MACD time series minus the MACD signal line indicates the slope of the price velocity curve at any point, i.e., the price acceleration. This acceleration is depicted by vertical bars (gray) on the MACD histogram as shown in the bottom chart on the previous page. Whenever the price accelerates, the MACD histogram is above zero. Acceleration is like a driver stepping on the gas to move. Whenever the price decelerates, the MACD histogram is below zero. Deceleration is like a driver pressing the brakes to slow down. The MACD histogram is significant because acceleration always changes before movement stops and reverses.

The MACD time series crosses its signal line when price acceleration is zero. The time to sell is when the MACD series is positive but reverses direction and then drops below its signal line. The histogram turns negative - in this case at age 21½, just after the true age 23 peak. The price has started to drop. The time to buy is when MACD is negative but reverses direction up and then crosses above its signal line; the histogram turns positive. The price has begun to rise. The MACD signal line cross marks a price reversal much sooner than a trailing price EMA cross does. To overcome the trailing average price time lag, track the price acceleration histogram instead.

Despite the delayed reactions that arise from trailing moving averages, MACD reliably identifies price reversals up after serious market declines. [Appel, ref 26] ***In summary, the MACD time series is a price speedometer that resembles RSI without the oversold/overbought limits. But the MACD histogram is unique because it is a separate gauge for the brakes and the gas designed to identify price reversals.***

The Percentage Price Oscillator (PPO) is based on relative instead of absolute prices, but is otherwise identical to MACD. Consequently, PPO charts of different investments are directly comparable in terms of percentage price changes instead of dollar per share price changes.

7.3 Volatility Indicators - Bollinger Bands (Std. Deviation) & Keltner Channels (Avg. True Range)

Volatility means a tendency to change quickly and unpredictably. Statistically, it is the extent of random fluctuations around a central value. An investment's past volatility can be quantified from its price history simply by its average true range or by its standard deviation instead.

Bollinger Bands quantify the normal spread of price fluctuations around a central value. A trailing simple moving average (SMA) based on closing prices from the previous 20 trading days typically establishes the middle price band. The standard deviation (σ) of these closing prices determines their normal variation relative to the average price. The upper band is routinely set by adding twice the 20-day price standard deviation to the middle band. The lower band is set by subtracting two standard deviations (2σ) from the middle band. Upper and lower bands based on +/- 2σ are statistically designed to enclose 95% of all prices presuming they are distributed evenly around the middle band. So, 19 of every 20 prices ultimately should lie between the bands.

When multiple prices touch or cross above the upper band, they are statistically high. Likewise, when multiple prices tag or cross below the lower band, they are statistically low. **Bollinger bands** expand and contract to display the price volatility, but they otherwise **resemble RSI oversold and overbought guidelines superimposed on the simple moving average price.**

Keltner Channels are similar to Bollinger Bands, but are based instead on a trailing exponential moving average (EMA) and a simple average true range (ATR) of prices. A 20-day EMA based on previous closing prices typically establishes the middle price band. The average true range of closing prices from the previous 10 days determines the variation relative to the average. The upper band is routinely set by adding twice the 10-day price ATR to the middle band. The lower band is set by subtracting twice the ATR from the middle band. Upper and lower bands are designed to enclose almost all prices.

A trading range is typically today's high price minus the low price. The true range extends this span to include the additional gap whenever yesterday's closing price lies outside of today's range. (See page 40 candlestick chart black arrows.) Thus, the true range is the largest difference between any two of these three prices. In theory, the true range shows the commitment or enthusiasm of traders. A large or increasing true range shows traders paid more or accepted less for a stock that day. A small or shrinking true range shows waning interest or apathy.

Compared to Bollinger Bands, Keltner Channels use a more responsive exponential moving average with a smoother, more constant ATR bandwidth. ***Keltner Channels resemble RSI oversold & overbought guidelines superimposed on the exponential moving average price.***

7.4 <u>Volume Indicators - PVO, Chaikin Money Flow, Volume by Price</u>

Supply and demand forces dictate price. When demand exceeds supply, the price goes up. When demand is less than supply, the price goes down. When demand balances supply, the price reaches equilibrium. Buyers create the demand, sellers provide the supply, and the price times the volume is how much money they exchange. Price or volume alone only tells half the story, but together they tell the whole truth. [Couling, ref 28]

The top chart below shows that daily volume ranged from 100,000 to 800,000 shares. Gray vertical bars show volume when the daily price increased; pink bars show volume when the price decreased. Based on a 200,000 average share volume and a $60 price/share, buyers and sellers would exchange $12 million of this small-cap stock during the trading session on a typical day, about 1% of the company value and shares outstanding.

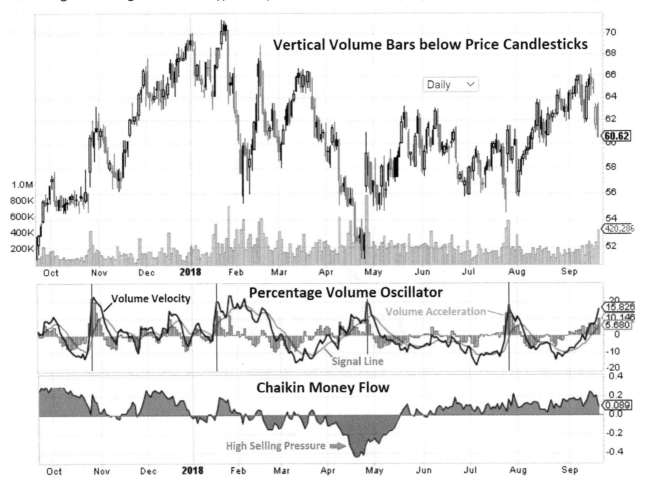

The Percentage Volume Oscillator (PVO) applies the very same numerical recipe to volume that the PPO applies to price. PVO is a *volume* speedometer with a histogram to show volume acceleration/deceleration. The middle chart on the previous page shows seasonal volume acceleration in October, January, April, and July as marked by purple vertical lines. This activity coincides with conference calls held to report quarterly earnings on 10/26, 1/15, 4/26, and 7/26.

The Chaikin Money Flow (CMF) is a 20-session running tally of stock or fund volume prorated by the respective strength of each closing price. When price closes at its high, the daily volume is added to the tally. When price closes at its low, the daily volume is subtracted. If price closes halfway between the high and low, the tally does not change. CMF is scaled from +1 for high buying pressure to -1 for high selling pressure. The last chart on the previous page shows selling pressure started to build in March and peaked in late April.

Volume by Price typically divides the closing price range spanning a specific time period into 12 equal vertical sections. The volume traded for each section is a horizontal bar. A gray bar denotes volume when the closing price moved up; a pink bar shows volume when the price went down. Long bars are high-volume price levels that mark resistance against higher prices or support against lower prices. A price breakout above a resistance level shows strong demand; a breakout below a support level indicates weak demand.

Volume is the effort and price is the reaction, so volume changes often lead or validate significant price changes. Volume also ultimately shows whether the market confirms or ignores financial news. A high-volume trading session coupled with a large price change typically indicates a major event that impacts the business outlook and triggers a news release. A surprising earnings report, a merger, or a management change may precipitate such a reaction. Volume measures trading activity as the total number of shares exchanged in multiple trades over time.

7.5 Breadth Indicators - AD Line, Hi-Lo Index, McClellan Volume Sum, % Stocks Above MA, BPI

Market breadth indicators quantify the collective status of many stocks in a group. Breadth indicators are often applied to the New York Stock Exchange (NYSE), NASDAQ, S&P, and DOW market indexes and sectors to assess the scope of strength or weakness. Before you elect to join the crowd or buck it instead, poll that audience first.

The Advance-Decline (AD) Line is a cumulative tally of advancing stocks minus declining stocks over time. Advancing stocks close at a higher price compared to the previous day, whereas declining stocks have a lower closing price. Regardless of its market capitalization size or volume traded, each advancing stock in the index adds 1 to the net advance each day, i.e. the "daily breadth". And each declining stock subtracts 1 from the daily count. A 9-day EMA is often used to smooth the tally of daily net advances.

When the price of a market index trends up or down, its AD Line quantifies how many stocks participate in this move. Because the market index price should increase when many stocks are advancing, a rising AD Line confirms the upward market trend. Likewise, a falling AD Line confirms a downward market trend. When the AD Line fails to confirm a market trend, they diverge. A bullish divergence occurs when the market trends down while the AD Line shows that many stocks are actually advancing. This anomaly suggests that the index price may reverse and go up. A bearish divergence occurs when the market trends up while the AD Line shows that most stocks are declining. This anomaly suggests that the index price may reverse and go down. The significance of any divergence between an indicator and price ultimately depends on the extent and duration.

The McClellan Volume Summation Index tracks the total *volume* of advancing stocks minus declining stocks. The McClellan Volume Oscillator is the 19-day EMA ("10% Trend") of daily net *volume* advances minus the 39-day EMA ("5% Trend"), i.e. the net advancing volume rate of change. The McClellan Volume Summation Index is simply a running total of the McClellan Volume Oscillator values. When more money has entered the market to broadly advance stock prices, the McClellan Volume Summation Index is high. When stock prices decline widely, more money has left the market and the McClellan Volume Summation Index is low.

The High-Low Index is a 10-day simple moving average (SMA) of the Record High Percent, which is the number of new daily 52-week highs divided by the total new 52-week highs plus 52-week lows. When the High-Low index equals 50, the number of 52-week highs equals the number of lows. A High-Low index of 30 corresponds to 3 new highs for every 7 new lows. This would imply a market index downtrend. A High-Low index of 70 means 7 new highs for every 3 new lows and would suggest a market index uptrend.

The Percent of Stocks Above Their Moving Average is typically based on a 50-day SMA in the short term and a 200-day SMA in the long term. Since an upward trend continues as long as the price stays above its moving average, this indicator shows the proportion of stocks in an index that are progressing.

The Bullish Percent Index (BPI) reports the percentage of stocks comprising an index or sector that are on Point & Figure chart buy signals. Each box on this chart denotes a *population* increment, typically a 2% change in how many stocks meet the P&F chart buy signal criteria. The 3-box reversal threshold here means that a 6% change triggers a new column to acknowledge that the qualifying population momentum has turned around.

When half the stocks qualify as P&F buys, the BPI is 50%. The index breadth is neutral. When 3 of every 10 stocks are P&F buys, the BPI is 30%. The index is considered oversold. A BPI equal to 0% means that no stocks in the entire index qualify as P&F buys. The index breadth can be no lower. When 7 out of 10 stocks are P&F buys, the BPI is 70%. The index is considered overbought. A BPI equal to 100% means that all stocks in the entire index qualify as a P&F buys. The index breadth can be no higher.

A Bullish Percent Index chart can be interpreted as a fixed playing field where buyers represent one team that moves the marker up and sellers represent the opposing team that moves the marker down (see the figure below). Sports such as football, basketball, soccer, and hockey all share this concept. A ball or puck serves to mark the field position. Whichever team has possession plays offense and moves the marker towards the goal. The opposing team plays defense until it gains possession. [Dorsey, ref 24]

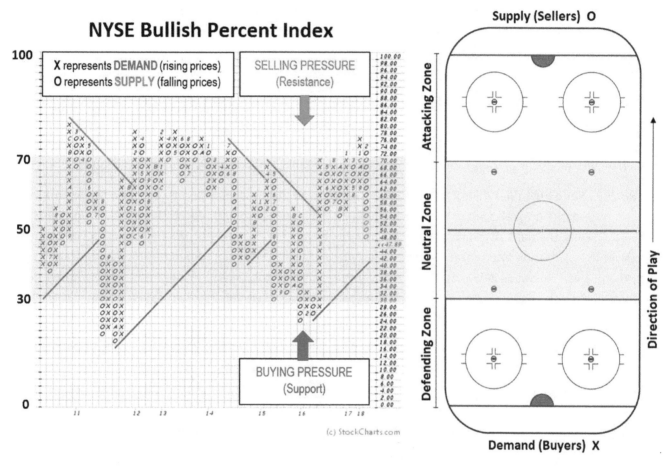

A rising column of X's on a BPI chart shows that broad demand is driving prices higher. Buyers control the puck. A falling column of O's shows that widespread supply is driving prices lower. Sellers control the puck. *A BPI chart reversal from one column to the next means losing or gaining possession, which triggers the strategic switch from offense to defense or vice versa.* The BPI value gives the puck's position.

When the puck is in the attacking zone but your team does not have possession, offense is no longer the proper strategy. Play defense (sell high at retail) when your opponent (sellers) has possession. Selling assets to raise cash when market risk is high reduces your risk. Likewise, when the puck is in the defending zone but your team has possession, defense is no longer the appropriate strategy. Play offense (buy low at wholesale) when your team (buyers) has possession. Buying when market risk is low utilizes cash to bet on potential future rewards.

BPI assesses market risk, not performance. Performance is accomplishment. Risk is exposure to possible loss. A high BPI means high risk, but prices could still rise. A low BPI implies low risk, but prices could fall.

7.6 <u>Sentiment Indicators - Put/Call Ratio, The VIX</u>

In finance, an option is a contract which gives the buyer the right to buy or sell the underlying investment asset at a specific "strike" price on or before a specific future "expiration" date. The option seller has the corresponding obligation to fulfill the transaction – to sell or buy the investment – if the buyer (i.e. owner) "exercises" the option. A "call" option gives its owner the right to buy at a specific price. So, a call owner speculates that the asset price will rise above the strike price before expiration. A "put" option gives its owner the right to sell at a specific price. So, a put owner speculates that the asset price will fall below the strike price before expiration. ***Like automobile and home owners who buy insurance for coverage against a potential loss, investors often buy stock index puts as insurance to hedge against a market decline.***

When the owner will profit from exercising an option, it is "in the money". An option is "at the money" when its strike price is equal to the current price of the underlying asset. A call is "out of the money" if the asset price is below the strike price. A put is "out of the money" if the asset price is above the strike price.

An expired option is like an insurance policy that terminates without any claim filed. Since statistics show that for every option exercised, three other options expire worthless, option buyers are actually wrong most of the time. Thus, betting contrary to the option buying crowd should hypothetically prove right most often.

The Put/Call Ratio quantifies the total puts traded divided by the total calls. When an equal number of puts and calls are traded, the put/call ratio is 1. Bearish and bullish sentiments balance each other. When more puts are traded than calls, the put/call ratio is above 1, and option buyers are bearish. But, when this pessimism becomes excessive, the contrarian interpretation suggests a potential bullish reversal. When more calls are traded than puts, the put/call ratio is below 1, and option buyers are bullish. But, when this optimism becomes excessive, the contrarian interpretation suggests caution against a stock market decline.

The Chicago Board Options Exchange (CBOE) is the largest U.S. options exchange with annual trading volume exceeding 1 billion contracts. CBOE offers options on over 2,200 companies, 22 stock indices, and 140 ETF's. CBOE compiles an Equity Put/Call Ratio, an Index Put/Call Ratio, and a combined Total Put/Call Ratio.

The CBOE Volatility Index (VIX) is a financial benchmark designed to forecast the variability of future market price movements. Every minute, the VIX estimates the expected volatility of the S&P 500 Index (SPX) over the next 30 days (one month) as implied by the bid/ask midpoint quotes for selected SPX options. Only options with more than 23 days and less than 37 days until the Friday SPX expiration date are used to calculate the VIX. Furthermore, only puts with strike prices at or below the forward SPX level and calls with strike prices at or above the forward SPX level are included. The quote for each selected SPX option is weighted based on its strike price and time to expiration. These weighted contributions are all added together and normalized to determine the expected volatility in percent per year. [CBOE, ref 29]

The forward SPX level is the median price forecast 30 days into the future. However, this forecast is disputed by option traders. Call buyers are convinced that the price is going higher within 30 days. They will pay now for the right to lock in a strike price surpassed going up. In contrast, put buyers are afraid that the price is going lower within 30 days. They will pay now for the right to lock in a strike price surpassed going down.

The VIX is typically computed from a few hundred put and call options, but the exact number of options used constantly varies. The strike price range for options having non-zero bids expands and contracts like a hand-held folding fan as volatility rises and falls. The VIX was specifically developed to measure this activity.

The figure below depicts the strike price range of S&P 500 puts and calls used to compute the VIX. The 30-day VIX time horizon is always bracketed by near term options that expire before then (shown by arrows) and next term options that expire beyond then (shown by diamonds). So, the range of strike prices at the horizon itself lies between these two extremes. The significance of each option's strike price is set by the bid/ask quote because investors ultimately voice their convictions by putting their money where their mouth is. Cheap options with extreme strike prices carry much less weight than expensive options with strike prices near the forward SPX level. Money talks.

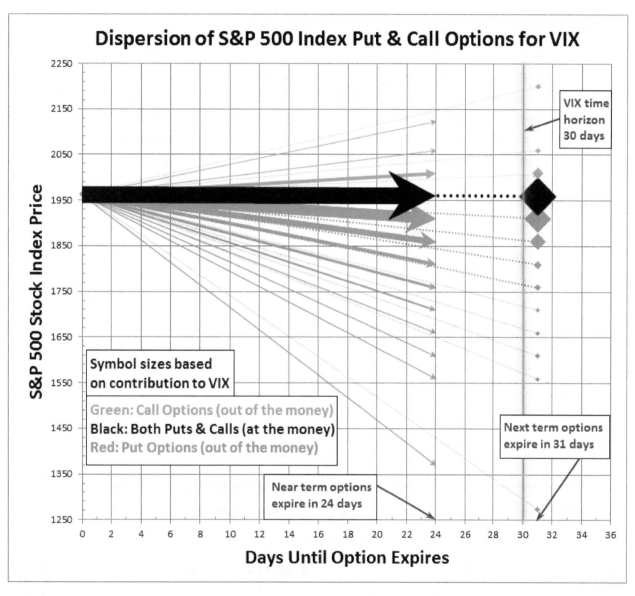

In this case, options forecast that in 30 days, the S&P 500 index will be between 1270 and 2200, probably between 1760 and 2060, and most likely near 1962, the forward index level. More precisely, the VIX translates the scatter of all these strike prices into a standard deviation of 13.7% per year. This value is equivalent to 4.0% per month. So, the VIX quantifies the dispersion of bets by the options market on the S&P 500 Index price 30 days from now. The VIX is often called the fear gauge for market sentiment because volatility makes investors anxious. ***A high VIX figure (above 25) shows market anxiety like a fully spread peacock tail rattling on display.***

Market sentiment may also be deduced from surveys instead of options. The American Association of Individual Investors (AAII) asks its members which way the stock market will go over the next six months. This poll tallies bullish, neutral, and bearish votes. The bull-bear spread has ranged from -54% to +63% and averaged 7.4% since 1987. The National Association of Active Investment Managers tracks the average exposure to US equity markets reported by its members. The NAAIM Exposure Index has ranged from -4% to +121% and averaged 65% since 2006. The Wall Street Sentiment report is a proprietary survey of traders and analysts that measures bullish and bearish opinions. These weekly surveys are all usually contrarian and can be tricky to interpret.

7.7 A Composite Market Indicator - The Fear & Greed Index

Of all the emotions that motivate investors, fear and greed are most often cited. Extreme fear can depress stock prices far too low. Extreme greed can bid up stock prices way too high. ***The CNN Money Fear & Greed Index consolidates seven equally weighted technical indicators into a single reading of emotion now driving the overall stock market.*** The Fear & Greed Index is scaled from 0 to 100. Readings below 25 represent Extreme Fear; 45 marks the transition from Fear to Neutral; 55 marks the boundary from Neutral to Greed; and readings above 75 mean Extreme Greed. [CNN Money, ref 30]

The seven individual indicators that comprise the Fear & Greed index are listed below.

- Stock Price Momentum: The difference between the S&P 500 stock index and its 125-day moving average

- Stock Price Strength: The percent of NYSE stocks hitting 52-week highs versus stocks at 52-week lows

- Stock Price Breadth: The McClellan Volume Summation Index of NYSE advancing versus declining volume

- Put and Call Options: The CBOE Put/Call ratio, the five trading day volume of bearish puts versus bullish calls

- Junk Bond Demand: The yield difference between riskier junk bonds and safer investment grade bonds

- Market Volatility: VIX, the S&P 500 Index standard deviation as implied by options that expire in 30 days

- Safe Haven Demand: The difference between stock versus US Treasury bond returns over 20 trading days

The current value of each indicator is compared to its range and activity over the last two years and scaled accordingly between 0 (Fear) and 100 (Greed). The Fear & Greed Index is an equal mix of all these indicators.

CHAPTER 8

8)   INTEGRATION: Putting It All Together

People routinely board all kinds of transportation vehicles without hesitation to get from one place to the next destination. Every investment is actually a financial vehicle, a dynamic Skinner box on wheels. The list below summarizes 10 fundamental and technical reasons to approve or reject a specific investment vehicle.

Fundamental Analysis

1) Consistently good past performance implies this vehicle can take me where I want to go. – *Visual Analysis*
2) The driver is qualified, skilled, and trustworthy. – *Management Evaluation*
3) The vehicle cost is commensurate with its output. – *Risk/Reward & Total Return*

Technical Analysis

1) Vehicle position is on the right side of centerline going in the right direction. – *Moving Average*
2) Vehicle position is within the rumble strips bordering the edges of the road. – *RSI*
3) Vehicle speedometer reads positive/negative. Fuel pedal or brakes depressed. – *MACD, PPO*
4) This vehicle's tracks show the route to my destination so far has been reasonably steady. – *Volatility*
5) This vehicle's passenger volume has been relatively high/low and supports the current price – *Volume*
6) Overall traffic is favorable/unfavorable: All vehicles are progressing/retreating. – *Breadth*
7) Most investors feel it's safe to leave home since the rewards now surpass the risk. – *Sentiment*

Fundamental analysis and technical analysis are complementary investing methods. Technical investors frequently apply fundamental analysis to identify the best businesses. Every business is a money-making machine. Learn how it works and how much it makes. Fundamental investors often use technical analysis to determine suitable entry and exit points. Every investment is a financial vehicle. Track its every move. To gain sound investments at a fair price, combine the best of both approaches, i.e. apply rational analysis.

In addition to all the fundamental and technical factors already noted, one more element should be incorporated into any investment approach. The financial news is a key trailing indicator all by itself. Although it always seems to come late, the news is still essential to put all the pieces together into proper context. Get the big picture clearly in mind before you risk any money. Each investment has its own story at any specific time. Your job as an investor is to learn that story before you decide what action is warranted. Business news sources include the Consumer News & Business Channel (CNBC), Reuters, and Bloomberg.

Notice whether the news either confirms or contradicts how investments actually behave. In a bull market, stocks don't go down on bad news even though they should. In a bear market, stocks don't go up on good news even though they should. The price and volume of investment transactions should ultimately match the news. Significant discrepancies hint that a change is forthcoming.

The following examples attempt to illustrate what can go right or wrong with any specific investment. Never confuse rising stock prices with financial genius. Forget about feeling smart. And remember that not every losing trade is a mistake. To become successful, you must accept responsibility regardless of the outcome. To paraphrase Warren Buffet once again:

> *You are not right because a thousand people agree with you. You are not wrong because a thousand people disagree with you. You are right because you have all the facts right, and your reasoning is right.*

"To those who use well what they are given, even more will be given, and they will have abundance."
> - Matthew 25:29

In 2018, Hasbro, Inc. was a large-cap international toy and game company whose products included G.I. Joe, Jenga, Monopoly, Nerf, Playskool, Scrabble, Tonka, and Transformers. Hasbro (HAS) also had established a strategic merchandising relationship with the Walt Disney Company for Marvel super heroes, Star Wars, and Toy Story products. However, in September 2017, the retail store company Toys "R" Us filed for bankruptcy and reported it would close about 200 stores in the United States. Later, on March 14, 2018, Toys "R" Us announced that all 800 US stores would be liquidated and closed. Hasbro's stock price fell from $110/share in July 2017 to $88/share by January 2018 and then $82/share by late March. Investor anxiety about how Hasbro could compensate for sales and earnings lost from Toys "R" Us stores was intense.

Hasbro – Fundamentals Thursday 3/22/18 (Based on review of Value Line data)

1) Sales growth: 7.5% past 10 years, 3.5% past 5 years, 7.0% forecast next 5 years
   Earnings growth: 12.0% past 10 years, 7.0% past 5 years, 11.0% forecast next 5 years
2) Profit Margins: Gradual rise from 9% to 11% over past 5 years
   Return on Equity: Steady at 15% over past 5 years
3) 3/22/2018 Price = $85.25/share, Earnings = $5.08/share, P/E = 16.8
   Estimated future low price $75, future high price $115, upside/downside = 29.75/10.25 = 2.9

Hasbro – Technicals Thursday 3/22/18 TOYS-R-US filed for bankruptcy Buy HAS @ $85.25/share

1) HAS 13% below 200-day simple moving average, September 2017 death cross not yet reversed
2) RSI reading 29: Oversold
3) PPO reading -2.9, histogram reading -0.95 but becoming less negative
4) Price currently below lower Keltner band
5) Daily volume higher than average for past few weeks and price has dropped 25% in 8 months
6) NYSE BPI at 59 in rising X column, Consumer Discretionary BPI at 43 in falling O column
7) VIX @ 20, but down from 35 in February 2018, Fear & Greed index about 12 (extreme fear)

Hasbro RSI, PPO, daily volume & candlestick chart with 200-day SMA, Keltner channels, & volume by price

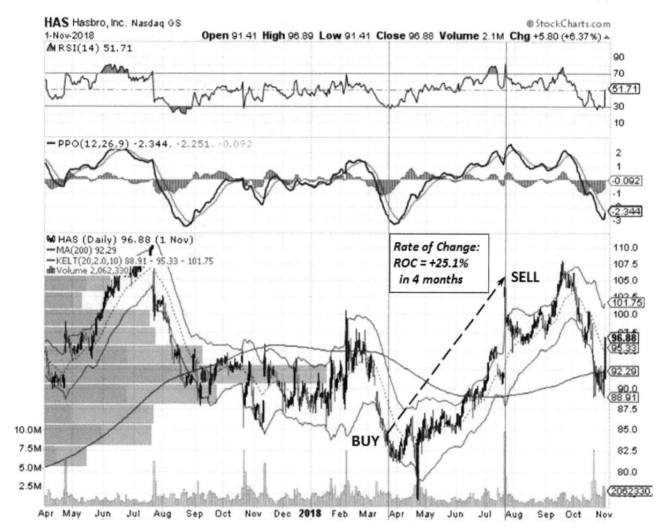

Hasbro – Technicals   Monday 7/23/2018   Hasbro posts great earnings report   Sell HAS @ $105.99/share

1) HAS 19% above 200-day simple moving average, July 2018 golden cross is positive progress
2) RSI reading 82: Overbought
3) PPO reading +2.0, histogram reading +0.37
4) Price just rocketed through upper Keltner band
5) Volume 10 times average drives price up 12% in one day
6) NYSE BPI at 60 in rising X column, Consumer Discretionary BPI at 55 in falling O column
7) VIX @ 12.6 and stable, Fear & Greed index about 60 (greed)

Total Return = ($20.74 Capital Gain + $0.63 May 2018 Dividend) / $85.25 purchase price = +25% in 4 months

Hasbro found other retailers, including Walmart, Target, and Amazon, who expanded their toy offerings after Toys 'R' Us folded. That transition took over a year. However, the initial investor reaction to Hasbro's 2018 second quarter sales and earnings report was so enthusiastic, the intraday price jumped up 12% to nearly $106/share on 10 times the normal daily volume.   The P/E was 21.3. This price was simply too good to pass up since the 25% gain in four months easily exceeded a 15% annual return target originally prescribed.

Cisco Systems (CSCO) went public in 1990. Its stock price was $0.10/share that year. In 1995, the price reached $1.25/share. By 1998, the price was over $12/share. In 2000, the price peaked at $64/share and the P/E ratio hit 120. On March 24, 2000, Cisco topped Microsoft to become the largest company in the world with a market capitalization of $580 billion. For ten straight years, Cisco was the goose that laid the golden egg.

Cisco long-term volume & candlestick chart with 200-day SMA, Keltner channels, & volume by price

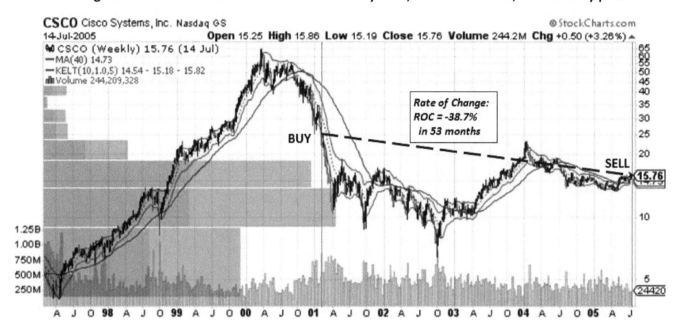

In retrospect, this date was ultimately the peak of irrational exuberance, i.e. the *dot.com* bubble. Although computers worldwide did not all crash after 11:59.59 PM on 12/31/1999, the massive buildup from the Y2K scare was about to unwind. On 2/6/2001, Cisco reported quarterly earnings per share 50% higher than one year earlier, but $0.01 less than analyst expectations. The next day, Cisco stated that quarterly revenue was expected to drop by 5%. A 16% workforce reduction was announced soon thereafter.

Cisco – Fundamentals Monday 2/7/01

1) Sales growth: 67% past 10 years, 25% conservatively forecast next 5 years
   Earnings growth: 53.0% past 10 years, +49% guidance for 2001, 25% forecast next 5 years
2) Profit Margins: Favorable over preceding 5 years
   Return on Equity: Favorable over preceding 5 years
3) 2/7/2001 Price = $25.72/share, Earnings = $0.41/share, P/E = 62.4
   Estimated future low price $19, future high price $92, upside/downside = 66.3/6.72 = 9.9

Cisco – Technicals Monday 2/7/01 Cisco lowers revenue guidance Buy CSCO @ $25.72/share

1) CSCO 45% below 200-day simple moving average, September 2000 death cross not yet reversed
2) RSI reading 33
3) PPO reading -5.4, histogram reading -1.3 and still falling from +2.5
4) Price breakdown through lower Keltner band
5) Volume triple normal average for previous 3 years, price down 62% in 10 months and 13% in 1 day

6) NASDAQ BPI at 50 in rising X column, Telecommunication BPI at 41 in falling O column

7) VIX @ 25, but down from 35 over 6 weeks

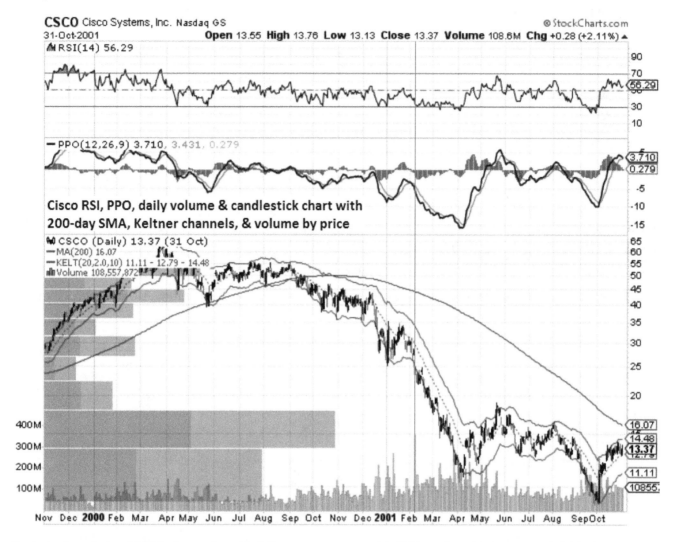

Cisco RSI, PPO, daily volume & candlestick chart with 200-day SMA, Keltner channels, & volume by price

Technical analysis of CSCO shows that the fall was not over on 2/7/2001. The PPO was -5 and the histogram was negative. The trading volume was three times normal on the same day the price dropped 13%. Lesson learned: do not try to catch a falling knife. Wait patiently for it to hit the ground first and then safely pick it up. Fortunately, CSCO was limited to 2.5% of the total investment portfolio when purchased in February 2001.

By the end of 2001, Cisco's stock price fell to $15/share. A year later, the price was just $11. Because the steady sales and earnings streams were broken, the P/E ratio fell to 28. Painfully simple math tells a depressing story: ***P/E x Earnings = Price***. The price in 2000: 120 x $0.53/share = $64/share. Price in 2002: 28 x $0.39/sh = $11/sh. This double jeopardy is shared by all fast growing, high P/E stocks. No earnings marshmallow, no premium P/E unit price. Beware! ***You swim in the deep end of the pool whenever you own a high P/E stock.***

Cisco's fall from grace was not unique. Iomega, JDS Uniphase, and many more stocks all went down. The PBHG technology and communications *fund* returned +112% in the fourth quarter of 1999 alone, but gave it all back 3 quarters later in 2000 with a -51% loss. If success means an investment doubles in five years, i.e. 20 quarters, then doubling in a single quarter instead implies a windfall much too good to last, and it didn't.

Cisco – Technicals   Thursday 7/14/05   P/E = 23   Final Capitulation   Sell CSCO @ $15.76/share

1) CSCO 7% above 200-day simple moving average
2) RSI reading 63
3) PPO reading +0.63, histogram now positive at +0.38
4) Price just below upper Keltner band
5) Volume near average, price down 35% in 18 months and flat for previous year
6) NASDAQ BPI at 51 in rising X column, Telecommunication BPI at 86 in rising X column
7) VIX @ 11

CSCO Total Return = (-$9.96 Capital Loss) / $25.72 purchase price = -39% in 53 months

OUTCOME 3 EXAMPLE: YOU MISSED A LOSS   "A penny saved is a penny earned."

On January 1, 2018, the iShares total US stock market ETF had gained 50% over the prior two years. Although it appeared to be overbought based on technical indicators for ticker ITOT, the market went up another 6% by February. The RSI hovered above 80, well above the overbought guideline. The price also ran beyond the upper Keltner band. After a 56% price run-up over 25 months, it takes discipline to wait even longer for a fair price.

RSI, PPO, daily volume & candlestick chart with 200-d SMA, Keltner channels, & volume by price for ticker ITOT

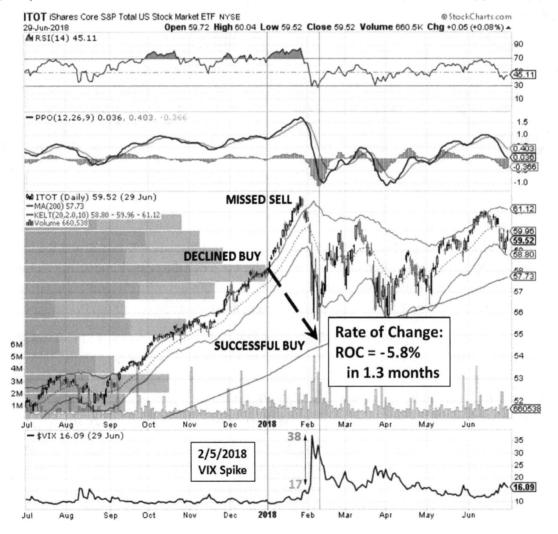

ITOT – Fundamentals   Tuesday 1/2/18

1) Earnings growth: 5% average annual growth since 2009
2) S&P 500 Index Price = 2790, S&P 500 Index P/E = 25.0

ITOT – Technicals   Tuesday 1/2/18   **Did not buy ITOT @ $58.15/share**

1) ITOT 9% above 200-day simple moving average
2) RSI reading 70
3) PPO reading +0.9, histogram reading just slightly negative
4) Price riding on upper Keltner band
5) Daily volume roughly twice average & price has climbed +9% in 4 months
6) NYSE BPI at 71 in rising X column
7) VIX @ 11, below 16 during all of 2017, Fear & Greed index about 65 (greed)

On Tuesday, January 30, the market began to reverse. Three days later, the U.S. jobs report showed that the unemployment rate was 4.1%, a 17-year low. However, wages grew at the fastest rate since 2009. Investors began to worry that the ideal balance of slow growth and mysteriously low inflation might end even though the U.S. economy was healthy. Besides the fear of higher inflation and multiple interest-rate increases by the Federal Reserve to come in 2018, more robust wage gains could eat into record-high corporate profits.

On Monday, February 5, the S&P 500 dropped 4%, giving back its 2018 year to date gains in the biggest one-day loss since 2011. As bonds and stocks sold off, the 10-year U.S. Treasury yield hit a four-year high of 2.85%, a dramatic swing from 2.4% to start 2018. The VIX doubled from 17 to 38 and created huge 95% losses ($3 billion) for investments (XIV, SVXY) specifically designed to generate extra income each day that market volatility stayed low. Although this apparently easy-money strategy of selling one-month VIX futures contracts had gained 200% during the prior 18 months, it was still always a long-term losing gamble. Inverse short-term VIX investors this day stepped in front of an oncoming train just to pick up a $20 bill. Forced to raise cash by liquidating assets to cover their losses, traders exacerbated a systemic selloff of U.S. stocks. Despite this turmoil, CNBC's Jim Cramer advised investors to treat the drop as a buying opportunity. The market closed down 5% for the week, the worst decline in two years. Volatility was back with a vengeance.

ITOT – Technicals   Friday 2/9/18   **Buy ITOT @ $54.80/share**

1) ITOT just 1% above 200-day simple moving average
2) RSI just above 30
3) PPO reading -0.8, histogram reading -1.1
4) Price well below lower Keltner band
5) Daily volume about 4 times average & price has dropped 12% in 10 trading days
6) NYSE BPI at 48 in falling O column
7) VIX @ 29, Fear & Greed index about 15 (extreme fear)

ITOT Total Return Saved = ($3.35 Capital Loss Avoided) / $58.15 starting price = +5.8% in 1.3 months

The price decline was quick and deep, but rebounded before trading ended that Friday. This long-term purchase established a new core position. ITOT is a well-diversified ETF comprised of over 3500 domestic stocks from all economic sectors.

In 2018, Clorox (CLX) was a large-cap international consumer product company whose brands included Clorox bleach, Brita water filters, Glad plastic bags, Kingsford charcoal, Liquid-Plumr drain opener, and surface cleaners like Formula 409, Pine-Sol, and Tilex. Despite solid financial results in 2017, Clorox still faced rising input costs and increased digital shopping by consumers. Thus, management vowed to streamline costs and invest in its established brands by emphasizing product innovation and digital marketing. CLX stock price fell as investors worried that demand for branded staples would stay weak as costs increased. Although Clorox announced a 14% dividend increase in February, pessimism grew In April 2018 when industry rival Procter & Gamble reported slow sales and falling prices for the quarter.

Clorox – Fundamentals   Tuesday 5/1/18

1)   Sales growth: 4% past 10 years, 2% past 5 years, 4% forecast next 5 years *(low growth)*
     Earnings growth: 5% past 10 years, 7.5% past 5 years, 8% forecast next 5 years *(low growth)*
2)   Profit Margins: Steady at 15% over past 5 years
     Return on Equity: *Not favorable; long-term debt = 70% total capitalization, debt > equity!*
3)   5/1/2018 Price = $111.55/share, Earnings = $5.45/share, P/E = 20.5
     Estimated future low price $101, future high price $155, upside/downside = 43.45/10.55 = 4.1

Clorox – Technicals   Tuesday 5/1/18   Did not buy CLX @ $112/share

1)   CLX 12% below 200-day simple moving average, February 2018 death cross not yet reversed
2)   RSI reading 36
3)   PPO reading -2.5, histogram reading -0.22 but becoming less negative
4)   Price crossed back above lower Keltner band
5)   Volume roughly twice average for past few weeks & price has dropped 20% in 22 weeks
6)   NYSE BPI at 52 in rising X column, Consumer Staples BPI at 41 in falling O column
7)   VIX @ 15, but down from 35 in February 2018, Fear & Greed index about 52 (neutral)

In early May 2018, Clorox reported third-quarter earnings and downgraded earnings for the full year. Later that month, the company announced a $2 billion stock repurchase program. In June 2018, Clorox shares rebounded 12% higher. Fourth-quarter sales and earnings reported in August 2018 both exceeded the previous-year figures. Sales were 2% below forecasts, but earnings beat estimates by 5%. Management also provided 2019 earnings guidance higher than Wall Street anticipated. First quarter sales and earnings reported after Halloween both beat analyst expectations; sales were up 4% and earnings were 11% higher than year earlier results. The stock price rose another 12% in November 2018.

Clorox RSI, PPO, daily volume & candlestick chart with 200-day SMA, Keltner channels, & volume by price

Clorox – Technicals Tuesday 11/27/18 P/E = 25.9 **Did not sell CLX @ $160/share**

1) CLX 23% above 200-day simple moving average
2) RSI reading 70
3) PPO reading +2.2, histogram reading +0.17
4) Price at upper Keltner band
5) Volume back to average & price has climbed 43% in 7 months
6) NYSE BPI at 58 in rising X column, Consumer Staples BPI at 56 in falling O column
7) VIX @ 12, Fear & Greed index about 75 (extreme greed)

Total Return Missed = ($48 Capital Gain + Dividends) / $112 purchase price = +42.9% in 7 months

In a sea of poor quarterly results from consumer goods competitors amid cost inflation and sluggish store sales, Clorox found success in its key businesses. The market rewarded Clorox shares. Modest sales and earnings growth combined with a higher P/E ratio gave a surprising 43% return in just 7 months.

Figuring total return for the previous four examples was simple, but a Quicken Investment Performance Report can automatically do this for all securities in your portfolio each day. Portfolio management decisions become much clearer with this level of understanding always at hand. The report below covers six purchases, four stock splits, and cash dividends for Paychex stock over ten years. The average total return was 14% per year.

Quicken Investment Performance Report for PAYX

Date	Action	Description	Investments	Returns	Avg Return	Additional Comments
6/5/1996	Buy	1.000 Paychex	$54.33			Initial Purchase - Ticker PAYX
7/1/1996	Buy	9.615 Paychex	$500.00			Additional Investment
8/6/1996	Buy	2.186 Paychex	$100.00			Additional Investment
9/3/1996	Buy	1.878 Paychex	$100.00			Additional Investment
2/3/1997	Buy	6.000 Paychex	$300.00			Additional Investment
5/21/1997	Sell	0.500 Paychex		$17.42		3 for 2 Stock Split - Cash for Fract Share
5/14/1998	Sell	0.500 Paychex		$17.92		3 for 2 Stock Split - Cash for Fract Share
9/10/1998	Buy	119.048 Paychex	$5,000.00			Additional Investment
5/16/1999	Sell	0.500 Paychex		$16.06		3 for 2 Stock Split - Cash for Fract Share
5/14/2000	Sell	0.500 Paychex		$15.79		3 for 2 Stock Split - Cash for Fract Share
8/8/2003	Sell	0.505 Paychex		$1.53		Sell Fract Share & Request Stock Certificate
11/17/2003	Div	Paychex		$46.44		Cash Dividend
2/17/2004	Div	Paychex		$46.56		Cash Dividend
5/17/2004	Div	Paychex		$46.56		Cash Dividend
8/16/2004	Div	Paychex		$46.56		Cash Dividend
11/15/2004	Div	Paychex		$50.44		Cash Dividend
2/15/2005	Div	Paychex		$50.44		Cash Dividend
5/16/2005	Div	Paychex		$50.44		Cash Dividend
8/15/2005	Div	Paychex		$50.44		Cash Dividend
11/15/2005	Div	Paychex		$62.08		Cash Dividend
2/15/2006	Div	Paychex		$62.08		Cash Dividend
4/3/2006	Sell	388.000 Paychex		$16,369.97		Final Sale
		TOTAL Paychex	**$6,054.33**	**$16,950.73**	**13.98%**	**Compound Annual Total Return, % per year**

CHAPTER 9

9)   WEALTH MANAGEMENT: Balancing The Trade-off Between Capital Preservation & Growth

Start with the end in mind. Invest periodic contributions that compound over time. Know yourself and manage your emotions. Choose fundamentally sound investments. Apply risk and money management to each one. Diversify assets over time by type, size, sector, and geography. Combine independent signals from multiple technical indicators to improve chances of success. Glean the financial news to clarify the big picture before acting on any investment. Integrate everything together into a rational approach.

If you accomplished all this, you would be well on your way to success. But the formula that builds a fortune demands greater understanding. No investor wins every time. Sequential investment gains create wealth, but losses destroy it. Balancing the trade-off between preserving wealth and growing it is absolutely crucial.

The longer you invest, the more likely you will experience situations that lead you to question your whole approach. The dot.com bubble, the global financial crisis, and the Coronavirus pandemic are three examples that have occurred over the past 25 years. One extreme is when your stop loss triggers fire sequentially like falling dominoes to sell every single position within days as prices plummet and leave your portfolio holding only cash. At the opposite end, you may find yourself completely invested and dreaming of a home equity loan or refinancing your mortgage to borrow even more money to invest right away before prices climb higher. You either can't take the pain any longer or you wish the party would never end. You are pushed to get either all out or more than all in. Your entire investing system is tested.

The answer to meet this challenge boils down to one single strategy. ***Always make the choice that will most likely succeed.*** Investing, like sports, is a game of percentages and not perfection. The best athletes take the highest percentage shots to have the best chance of winning. This approach earns championships each season even though many shots do not score points and some losses still occur. To quote famous football coach Vince Lombardi, "Winning is not a sometime thing; it's an all time thing. You don't win once in a while. You don't do things right once in a while, you do them right all the time. Winning is a habit."

Economics under risk is actually similar to the evolution of biological populations. [Stearns, ref 31] Consecutive gains in wealth correspond to reproductive success each generation. Economic fortune is akin to evolutionary fitness. Fitness is the ability of a population to reproduce, i.e. to maintain or increase its numbers in succeeding generations. Because populations and economic wealth multiply over time, the geometric mean gain is the true measure of fitness for each one. In addition, high temporary deviations reduce long-term fitness and increase the probability of extinction. In other words, consistency promotes fitness and lowers the risk of dying out.

Nothing indicates fitness better than perennial stamina. Every investment approach fit for lasting success consistently compounds growth and minimizes risk time after time. Smart investors constantly seek more growth and less risk, but everyone has their own opinion about how much risk to bear for the corresponding reward. Still, guidelines that provide a basis to make sound investment decisions do exist. The consequences of ignoring or violating these guidelines can be disastrous. As stated in Chapter 5, when investments are held unconditionally and never sold, the total potential portfolio loss is limited by the cash position size. With no cash, a fully invested portfolio can amount to an all or nothing bet. Losing it all is indeed possible. You could soon be demoted back to square one.

Navigating the long journey to financial independence can be risky business. Aim for steady progress without backtracking. Your best approach depends on the true caliber of your investments and your own temperament.

9.1 <u>The Kelly Optimum Bet Fraction</u>

Imagine a simple bet that doubles your total wealth if you win, but takes it all away if you lose. You would bet everything if you always win. You would bet nothing if you always lose. As long as you keep betting and winning, your wealth will grow by 100% per bet. However, lose just once, and then the game is over.   Your wealth is all gone. So, repeating this all or nothing bet soon leads to ruin unless winning is 100% guaranteed.

Although losing $500,000 on a double or nothing bet might be a fatal mistake, losing $5 on the same bet is just a mosquito bite. So, what if you bet only *PART* of total wealth each time? (Like a Daily Double on Jeopardy, the TV game show.) What fraction should you bet and how much would you gain or lose? Your fortune hinges on this simple, but critical question. In short, to maximize long term growth of wealth, set the bet size, f, to be your edge divided by the payoff odds. The edge is simply the bet's expected value, which must be positive or no bet is made. Since the payoff odds are 1:1, the optimum bet size for this wager is the probability of winning minus the probability of losing (as shown in Appendix C). [Kelly, ref 32] ***Bet more when your winning edge is higher.***

$$f_{Kelly} = (\text{Payoff 1} \times \text{Probability 1} + \text{Payoff 2} \times \text{Probability 2}) / \text{Payoff Odds}$$

$$f_{Kelly} = (+1 * P_{win} - 1 * P_{lose}) / 1 = P_{win} - P_{lose}$$

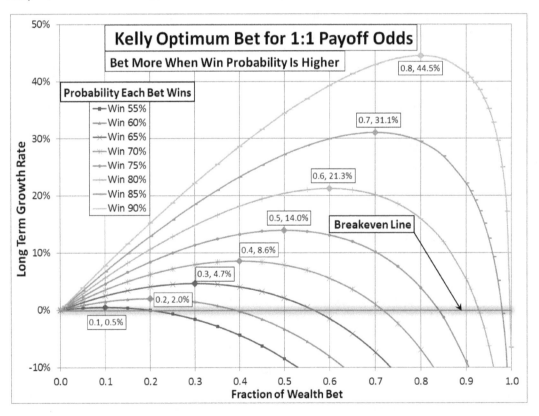

For example, if the probability of winning is 55%, then the probability of losing is 45% and the ideal bet is 10% (1/10) of total wealth. Although each single bet either gains +10% or loses -10% of total wealth, the overall long-term growth rate is +0.5% per bet. If the probability of winning is 75%, then the ideal bet size is 50% (1/2) of wealth. Now each single bet returns +50% or -50% of wealth and the long-term growth rate is +14% per bet. For a 90% winning probability, bet 80% (4/5) of wealth. A single bet returns +80% or -80% of wealth and the long-term growth rate is then +44% per bet.

No matter how favorable any bet is, its outcome can still be a loss. Systematically betting more than the true probabilities dictate can lead to negative growth rates and ultimately cause bankruptcy. For example, if the winning probability is 65%, repeatedly betting 65% of wealth instead of 30% triggers a 4% overall loss per bet. ***So, an investor can still go broke making positive expected value bets just by betting too much at once.***

This progression of repeated bets with uncertain outcomes is reminiscent of the ancient Indian board game, Snakes & Ladders. The best known U.S. edition is Chutes & Ladders, by Milton Bradley. Each player rolls a single cube of dice to randomly specify how many squares to advance on each move. Landing on a square at the top of a chute slides a player further back (a loss). Landing at a ladder base boosts a player further ahead (a gain). It takes 39 moves on average to reach square 100, that is, 2.55 squares forward per move. But, the average roll is 3.50 instead. The figure below shows a very lucky sequence that ends on square 100 in just 10 moves.

Very lucky scenario of "Chutes & Ladders" (Milton Bradley)

Roll sequence: 4, 2, 3, 5, 3, 2, 6, 5, 1, 4   Square Progression: 14, 6, 31, 44, 26. 84, 90, 75, 76, 100

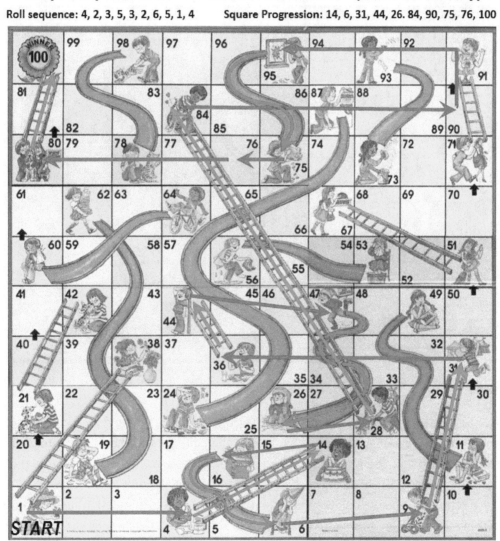

This winning 10-move scenario is not likely to be repeated often since over 60 million different 10-roll sequences are possible. In addition, if the board was different, the exact same roll sequence would not give the same results even though the same game is being played. For example, the alternate outcome on the next page ends on square 57 instead of 100. This is clearly less progress by comparison, but still better than expected. So, the outcome ultimately depends not only on the roll sequence, but on the underlying snakes (losses) and ladders (gains) that comprise the board as well. In any case, another name for this game would be "Losses & Gains".

Same game, different board - an alternate outcome of Snakes & Ladders
Roll Sequence: 4, 2, 3, 5, 3, 2, 6, 5, 1, 4   Square Progression: 4, 6, 9, 14, 17, 38, 22, 27, 53, 57

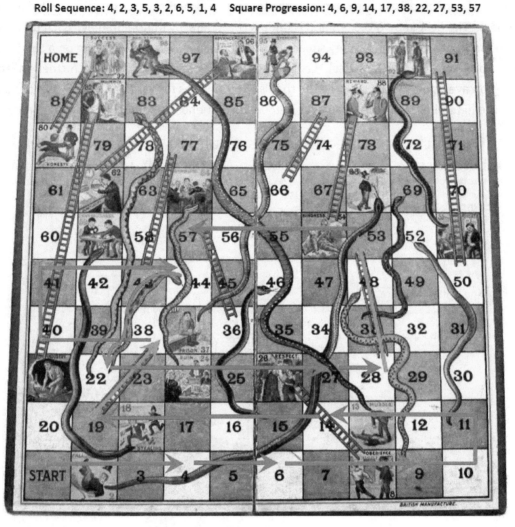

9.2 Wealth Distribution of Compounded Variable Investments

Individual random events are by definition unpredictable, but often the frequency of different outcomes over numerous events is predictable. Beyond even-payoff bets, the Kelly strategy has also been applied to portfolio investment growth models that use hundreds of decision points (sequential bets) and thousands of projected scenarios (progression outcomes). Instead of rolling dice and counting squares on a board to complete each game, however, a computer executes all the details. These Monte Carlo simulation results can be statistically summarized to show the spectrum of wealth trajectories for the optimal, full Kelly bet as well as smaller or larger wagers. The statistics show how effectively each specific bet size ultimately avoids losses and builds wealth based on the underlying investment probabilities and payoffs. No one size fits all investors because they have different risk aversion attitudes, but *quantifying the chances and magnitude of potential losses versus gains helps reveal the difference between a reasonable risk and a reckless one.*

For instance, suppose the investment sequence includes five distinct possibilities, each with a different winning probability and payoff odds as shown below. [Ziemba, ref 33]

Prospective Investment	Win Probability	Payoff Odds	Expected Value	Kelly Bet
1	57.0%	1-1	0.14	0.140
2	38.0%	2-1	0.14	0.070
3	28.5%	3-1	0.14	0.047
4	22.8%	4-1	0.14	0.035
5	19.0%	5-1	0.14	0.028

The expected value of each investment is readily computed using the equation below.

$$\text{Expected Value} = (\text{Payoff 1} \times \text{Probability 1} + \text{Payoff 2} \times \text{Probability 2}) = (\text{Odds} \times P_{win} - 1 \times P_{lose})$$

These prospective investments all have the same +0.14 expected value or edge. But, the ones having higher payoff odds have progressively lower winning probabilities. Because the Kelly optimum bet fraction is the expected value divided by the payoff odds, the Kelly strategy bets less not only when the expected value is lower, but also when the payoff odds are higher. ***Always bet less on long shots with the same expected value.***

$$f_{Kelly} = \text{Expected Value} / \text{Odds} = (\text{Odds} \times P_{win} - 1 \times P_{lose}) / \text{Odds}$$

While each single bet either loses the fraction wagered or wins that wager times its payoff, the long-term overall growth rate is +0.2% to 1% per bet since winning payoffs ultimately exceed losses for each prospect.

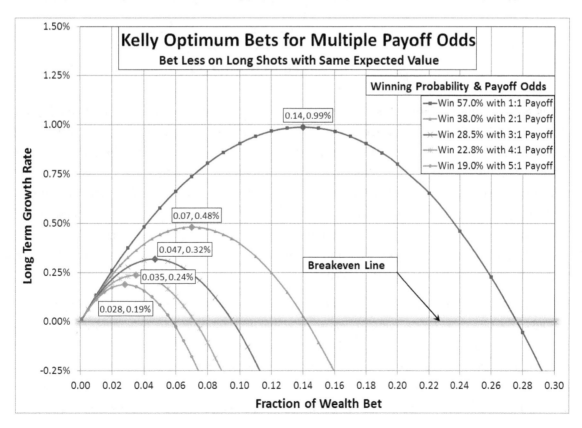

Ziemba randomly chose these five investments 10%, 30%, 30%, 20%, and 10% of the time, respectively, for 700 consecutive bets each won or lost based on its probability. For each win, wealth multiplied by (1+ f*Odds). For each loss, the wealth decay multiple was (1-f). This procedure was repeated for 2,000 scenarios all with the bet size, f, set relative to the Kelly fraction. The figure below shows the final wealth attained in six cases.

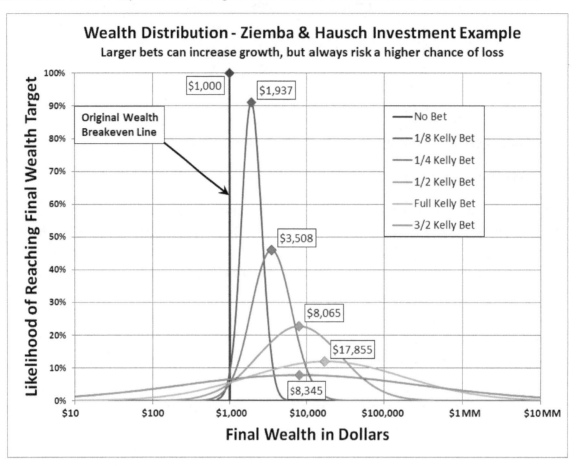

Betting nothing each time guarantees no loss, but also offers no chance of gain beyond the $1,000 original wealth. Betting just 1/8 the full Kelly fraction increases the median wealth to $1,937, but also creates a 1.2% chance that final wealth will fall shy of $1,000. By definition, final wealth is below the median for half of the scenarios but above the median for the other half. The 1/4 Kelly bet raises the median wealth to $3,508, but further increases the chance of loss to 1.8%. The 1/2 Kelly bet is more aggressive, boosting the median to $8,065, while giving a 4.3% chance of loss. The full Kelly bet generates the highest median final wealth, $17,855, but the likelihood of a loss is over 10%. The 3/2 Kelly bet has a whopping 27% chance of loss and only offers $8,345 median wealth. The area beneath the tail of each curve on the left side of the $1,000 breakeven line represents the likelihood of lost wealth after 700 bets.

Although any specific outcome depends on how many bets are actually won and lost, increasing the fraction bet always spreads the outcome range wider because the wagers compounded are larger, win or lose. Also, increasing the fraction bet beyond the Kelly limit reduces the median wealth, but increasing the fraction bet up to the Kelly limit raises the median wealth. So, ***betting more helps if the median goes up without much greater chance of loss.*** But, betting more hurts if the chance of loss becomes too great even if the median moves higher. ***When loss becomes more likely AND the median moves lower, betting more is reckless.***

Because each bet has a random outcome, the final wealth actually realized can't be predicted with certainty. However, it can be characterized by two expectations, namely the mean value and its standard deviation. These statistical measures for the Ziemba & Hausch wealth distribution curves are shown in the two figures below. The mean value is the expected final wealth. The standard deviation indicates the dispersion of possible values above and below the mean. The greater the standard deviation, the further away final wealth may actually be from the mean, and thus losing wealth becomes more likely instead of building it as intended. Relative to the starting wealth, increasing the bet size below the full Kelly fraction raises the final wealth up-side reward. But, increasing the bet size beyond the full Kelly fraction increases the down-side penalty. It is 68% likely that final wealth will be within one standard deviation above or below the mean wealth.

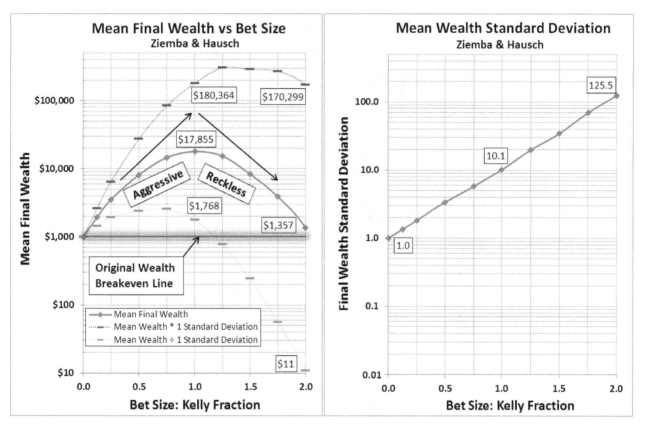

The same statistics apply to both the average outcome of a past event and the expected value of an uncertain future event. The mean value of a past series is called its average. The mean of an uncertain future event, depicted by a probability distribution, is called its expected value. The median of a probability distribution is its midpoint value. The mean and the median are generally two different ways to measure the center. But, because a statistically normal distribution is symmetric, the mean value in this case occurs at the median.

Investors can visualize the distribution of portfolio growth scenarios by witnessing a cascade of beads fall down a Galton Board or the Eames probability machine as seen during the 1964 New York World's Fair. This device is a vertical board with pegs symmetrically arranged in a quincunx pattern to form interleaved rows as pictured on the next page. Thousands of beads are introduced at the top. Each one drops by gravity until it hits a peg and is deflected either left or right with equal probability. At the end of its zigzag path through all the pegs, each bead ultimately lands in a bin. Several bins segregate all the beads into columns. The height of each column is proportional to the number of different paths that lead to each bin.

Most beads land near the center because they have an equal chance of going left or right every step down. If beads move one step horizontally per row, reaching a bin ten steps to the right or left after ten rows would be as likely as flipping a coin to tally ten straight heads or tails. Tilting the board to the right shifts the distribution in that direction because falling right at each peg (a gain) is now more probable than falling left (a loss).

Each peg encountered represents a single bet or investment portfolio decision point. Each bead portrays a history of many successive bets won or lost, i.e. an investor lifetime. The board depicts all the prospective investment probabilities. Replacing the beads with fine sand instead would reduce the extent of deflection left or right every step and narrow the distribution. This is akin to making tiny consecutive bets like 1/8 Kelly.

The investment payoff odds and probabilities presented by Ziemba & Hausch are rarely defined so clearly in practice. So, consider another example with different prospective investments. Presume a single risky asset that has a +12.5% annual mean return, R, uniformly distributed between -25% and +50%. Also assume that un-invested wealth can earn interest with no risk of loss and that more money can be borrowed by paying the same interest rate, r. If λ is the proportion of wealth invested in the risky asset, then λ = 2.4 means that $1.40 is borrowed for each $1 of current wealth and $2.40 is then invested in the risky asset. If λ = 0.4, then no money is borrowed and $0.40 is invested for each $1 of current wealth while $0.60 earns interest. [MacLean, ref 34]

This uniform return example by Bicksler & Thorp is different from Ziemba & Hausch in two respects. First, instead of individual investment prospects with fixed probabilities and payoff odds, the prospective investment has been characterized by an average one-year return with a probability range. This approach consolidates individual bets from shorter time frames and/or different investments. This emphasizes the risk and reward for managing an entire investment portfolio instead of just considering the losses and gains of each specific trade. Second, the fraction invested each year can also be more than the investor's wealth because additional money can be borrowed and invested. ***Using borrowed money to acquire an investment asset is called financial leverage.*** Brokers lend money to investors who pledge their own stocks as collateral in a margin account.

When the interest rate earned on savings and paid on borrowed money is 0% per year, the Kelly optimum bet fraction corresponds to $\lambda = 2.87$. This means that $1.87 is borrowed for each $1 of current wealth and $2.87 is then invested in the risky asset. Uniformly distributed investment returns between -25% and +50% were randomly selected for 40 consecutive years. Each year, wealth multiplied by $[1+r+\lambda*(R-r)]$, the annual geometric return. This procedure was repeated for 3,000 scenarios all with the bet size, f, set relative to the Kelly fraction. The figure below shows the final wealth attained in five cases.

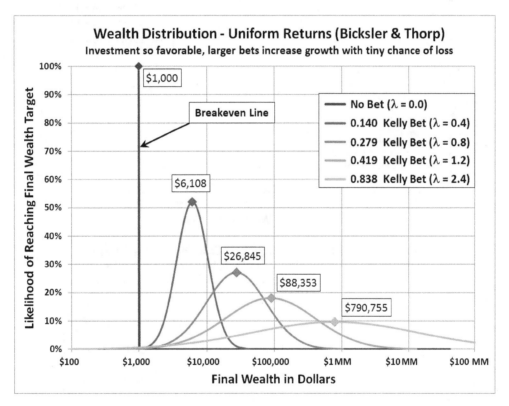

Once again, betting nothing each time guarantees no loss, but also offers no chance of gain beyond the $1,000 original wealth. However, that would be a shame in this case because investment is so favorable that larger bets increase growth with only tiny chances of loss. Betting just 0.140 the full Kelly fraction increases the median wealth to $6,108 without creating any significant chance that final wealth will fall shy of $1,000. The 0.279 Kelly bet raises the median wealth to $26,845, but only increases the chance of loss to 0.02%. The 0.419 Kelly bet is more aggressive, boosting the median to $88,353, while giving only a 0.2% chance of loss. The 0.838 Kelly bet generates the highest median final wealth, $790,755, but the likelihood of a loss is still just 1%. This playing field clearly favors investing. The rewards easily outweigh the risks.

The Bicksler & Thorp uniform return example is probably too good to be true. It would be more realistic to base calculations on two assets, namely U.S. equities and U.S. Treasury bills. Between 1926 and 2001, U.S. equities returned 10.2% with a 20.3% annual standard deviation; U.S. Treasury bills returned 3.9% with 0% standard deviation. [Siegel, ref 35] Based on these figures, the Kelly optimum bet fraction now corresponds to λ = 1.53. This means that $0.53 is borrowed for each $1 of current wealth and $1.53 is then invested in the risky asset. Normally distributed investment returns were randomly selected for 40 consecutive years. Each year, wealth multiplied by [1+r+λ*(R-r)], the annual geometric return. This procedure was repeated for 3,000 scenarios all with the bet size, f, set relative to the Kelly fraction. The first chart below indicates the final wealth attained in several cases.

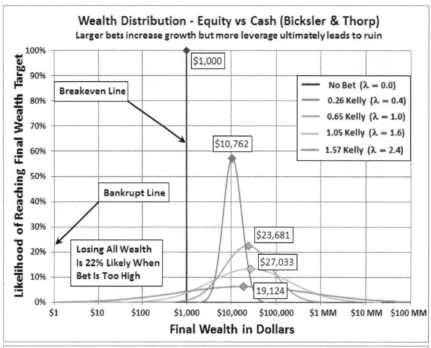

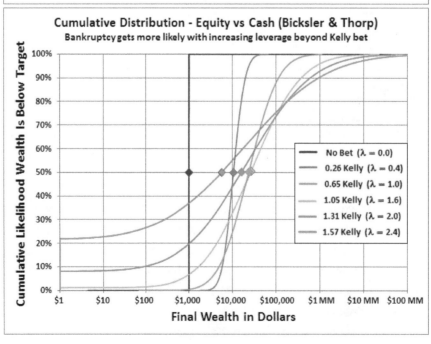

Betting nothing each time still guarantees the $1,000 original wealth with no loss or gain. Betting 0.26 the full Kelly fraction increases the median wealth to $10,762 with no significant chance that final wealth will fall shy of $1,000. **The 0.65 Kelly bet raises median wealth to $23,681, but the chance of loss remains below 1%.** The 1.05 Kelly bet boosts the median to $27,033, but gives a 7% chance of loss. The 1.57 Kelly bet appears to generate a $19,124 median final wealth, but the likelihood of a loss balloons to 37%.

Notice that the investment playing field has clearly shifted relative to the original wealth breakeven line. The same amount of leverage has become a much riskier proposition because the risky asset mean return is less (10.2% versus 12.5%) and the cost of borrowing money is more (3.9% versus 0%). Since the optimal Kelly bet has dropped from $\lambda = 2.87$ to $\lambda = 1.53$, the highly leveraged $\lambda = 2.4$ bet size is now well beyond the Kelly limit. Consequently, the risk of loss that first got serious at the breakeven line has now become fatal at the bankrupt line where wealth is gone.

For each bet size, the cumulative distribution of wealth on the previous page shows the proportion of scenarios less than or equal to any specific final wealth value. This figure more clearly exposes the consequences of over-betting. The 1.05 Kelly bet has a 7% chance of loss, including a 1% chance of ending with $1 or less, i.e. going bankrupt. The 1.31 Kelly bet has a 20% chance of losing wealth, including an 8% chance of going broke. Not only does the 1.57 Kelly bet have a 37% chance of losing wealth, but bankruptcy is actually 22% likely and drops the true median wealth down to $6000. In this case, the risks easily outweigh the rewards. Some famous hedge funds have gone bust by over-betting with leverage during a fatal losing streak.

The investment examples by Ziemba & Hausch and Bicksler & Thorp produced final wealth distributions that had one symmetrical peak for each bet size. These curves are statistically normal distributions plotted on a logarithmic scale. This phenomenon is no coincidence. Whenever investments produce earnings that are reinvested, those earnings then generate future earnings. This snowball effect is called compounding and commonly leads to growth represented by a logarithmic normal distribution with a mean value and standard deviation as shown in the figure below.

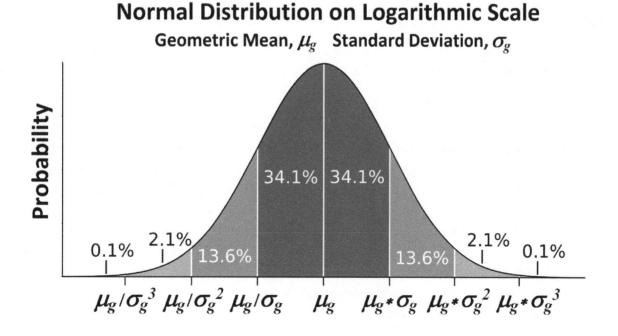

Normal Distribution on Logarithmic Scale
Geometric Mean, μ_g Standard Deviation, σ_g

The geometric mean of two numbers is the square root of their product. The geometric mean of three numbers is the cube root of their product. The geometric mean of final wealth for 2,000 or 3,000 investment scenarios is computed likewise. For each bet size, μ_g, is the geometric mean final wealth for all investment scenarios. The standard deviation, σ_g, is a multiple of μ_g that quantifies the variation of final wealth outcomes on a logarithmic scale.

One Equity versus Cash (Bicksler & Thorp) bet size is special because it represents a fully invested portfolio with no leverage, namely, the 0.65 Kelly bet (λ = 1.0). This bet has a median final wealth 23.68 times the original wealth (μ_g = 23.68), and a 3.43 standard deviation (σ_g = 3.43). This indicates a 50 % chance that wealth (without any periodic contributions) will multiply by at least 23.68 over 40 years. On the downside, this bet implies a 15.8% chance wealth will multiply by 23.68/3.43 = 6.90 or less, a 2.2% chance wealth will multiply by 23.68/3.43/3.43 = 2.01 or less, and just a 0.1% chance wealth will multiply by 23.68/3.43/3.43/3.43 = 0.59 or less. These figures verify the historical success of a 40-year buy and hold investment strategy based on a diversified U.S. stock portfolio between 1926 and 2001. The long-term rewards easily outweighed the risks in this situation. Nearly all such investors successfully built wealth.

The Kelly capital growth strategy is an attractive approach to wealth creation. The Kelly criterion maximizes the geometric mean of investment returns compounded over time. The geometric mean indicates the average long-term growth rate of wealth. The Kelly optimum bet size minimizes the time to reach long term investment goals and defines the boundary between aggressive investing and reckless risk-taking. However, ***although no other strategy ultimately builds more wealth in less time, full Kelly bets are large and can be risky in the short-term.*** Significant wealth can be lost by a sequence of unprofitable bets even though investment opportunities may be quite favorable. Betting 3/4, 1/2, or 1/4 of the full Kelly fraction instead is one approach to reducing the downside risk at the expense of accepting less growth. Consequently, investors who stand more to lose are typically advised to hold less stock and more cash instead. The Kelly strategy sometimes suggests investing and risking borrowed money to maximize long-term growth. However, this ***use of leverage significantly increases the chance of going broke in the short-term.***

9.3 *Risk Tolerance: A Bird in the Hand or Two in the Bush*

Suppose you have the choice of $1,000 guaranteed or a 50/50 gamble that pays $2,000 or nothing. Since the gamble has a $1,000 expected value, you may be indifferent to either choice, i.e. risk neutral.

Expected value = $2,000 x (1/2) + $0 x (1/2) = $1,000

But, if you don't like risk, you would choose the certain payment instead of the gamble. In fact, you would accept less than the expected value, say $900, just to lock in a sure thing. In essence, you have paid a $100 insurance premium to eliminate the risk of getting nothing. So, you sleep better at night. However, if you love risk, you would choose the gamble instead of the certain payment. In fact, you must be guaranteed more than the expected value, say $1,100, to give up your shot at $2,000. Basically, someone else has paid you an extra $100 to eliminate their risk of losing $2,000. So, you intend to eat well. The risk loving extreme always makes the bet. The risk adverse extreme never makes the bet and always takes the guaranteed payout instead. The minimum payout you would accept instead of the gamble is called the certainty equivalent. Your risk premium is the expected value minus the certainty equivalent. [Wikipedia, ref 36] Note that if the $1,000 was already yours in the first place, this choice amounts to betting double or nothing versus not gambling.

Choice Under Risk: "Deal or No Deal"

The TV game show "Deal or No Deal" explores behavioral economics. After each round, the "Banker" offers to buy the contestant's briefcase based on the cash values inside unopened briefcases. The 26 cash values initially in play range from $0.01 to $1,000,000 and are randomly eliminated as each briefcase is opened to reveal the next amount removed from the board. Rejecting an offer will force more cases to be opened in the next round and change the board for better or worse. Accepting an offer ends the game. How risk affects the decisions contestants make is not always obvious. [Forelle, ref 37]

For example, in one particular game, the last five unopened cases held $10, $10,000, $200,000, $400,000, and $500,000, respectively. The contestant accepted the banker's $165,000 round 6 offer.

The expected value of all five unopened briefcases was actually $222,002.

Expected value = Payoff 1 x Probability 1 + Payoff 2 x Probability 2 + … + Payoff 5 x Probability 5

Expected value = $10 x (1/5) + $10,000 x (1/5) + $200,000 x (1/5) + $400,000 x (1/5) + $500,000 x (1/5)

Expected value = $222,002

This implies the contestant paid a huge risk premium that amounts to 26% of the expected value.

Risk premium = Expected value − Certainty Equivalent = $222,002 - $165,000 = $57,002

This choice seems senseless until one more factor is considered. What if the decision was based on how the money could be used instead of its face value? The $165,000 could go a long way towards purchasing a new house or starting a new business. Maybe this utility justifies a "better safe than sorry" attitude here. Perhaps expected value is not the true decision basis actually followed under these circumstances.

9.4 Risk is Relative: The Utility of Wealth

More money is better. Economic utility is the satisfaction that money can buy. As wealth changes, its utility changes at a rate called the marginal utility. The marginal utility of wealth is always positive. More money always provides more utility, but at an ever decreasing rate. As wealth increases, the change in its marginal utility is always negative. ***So, the wealthier you are, the less additional utility you get from more money.***

For example, suppose one day you were surprised to discover an extra $1,000. Your reaction would depend on how much wealth you already had. If you originally had only $1,000 and gained another $1,000, you would be ecstatic because you now have twice as much. If you had $1,000 in the bank and lost $1,000, you would be devastated because you are now bankrupt. But had you started with $10,000, your feelings would be more tempered. You would still be happy with a $1,000 gain, but it is now 10% more instead of twice as much. You would still be dejected by a $1,000 loss, but you would be down just 10% instead of bankrupt. If you originally had $100,000 and lost or gained another $1,000, it would represent just a 1% change. Had you started with $1,000,000, you might not even notice a $1,000 change. So, the true value of your next $1,000 gained or lost is relative. [Bernoulli, ref 38]

Two features define a plot of economic utility as a function of wealth, namely, the slope and the curvature. The slope is always positive because it denotes the marginal utility. The curvature is concave because marginal utility always declines at an ever decreasing rate. The utility plot on the next page expresses these features.

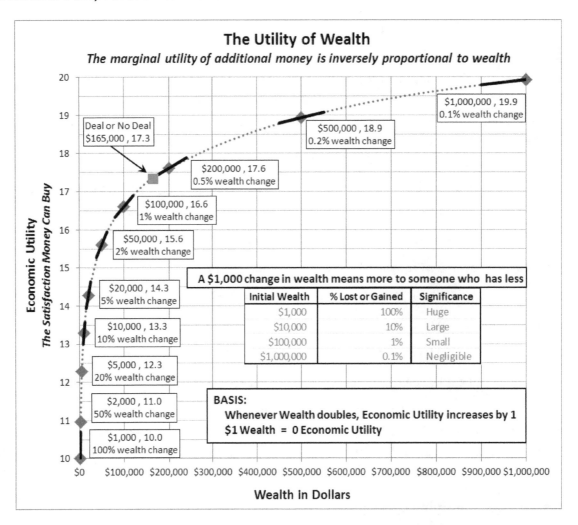

The decreasing marginal utility of increasing wealth is depicted by the black line segments that show how the (positive) slope changes from nearly vertical at low wealth points to nearly horizontal at high wealth points.

Economic utility provides a new basis to reassess the previous "Deal or No Deal" example. [Cramton, ref 39] The utility of the banker's $165,000 offer was 17.3 based on the plot above. But, the expected value of utility for all five unopened briefcases was actually 14.4.

Expected utility = Utility 1 x Probability 1 + Utility 2 x Probability 2 + ... + Utility 5 x Probability 5

Expected utility = 3.3 x (1/5) + 13.3 x (1/5) + 17.6 x (1/5) + 18.6 x (1/5) + 18.9 x (1/5)

Expected utility = 14.4

Since the banker's offer had a guaranteed utility significantly higher than expected utility of the unopened briefcases, the contestant made a personally satisfying choice based on the utility that $165,000 could buy.

9.5 Risk Aversion & Utility Function Curvature

Most people agree that as wealth increases, its marginal utility decreases. However, one size does not fit all. Different individuals can have much different opinions on exactly how marginal utility changes with wealth. For example, the figure on the next page compares the utility functions that characterize several different investors.

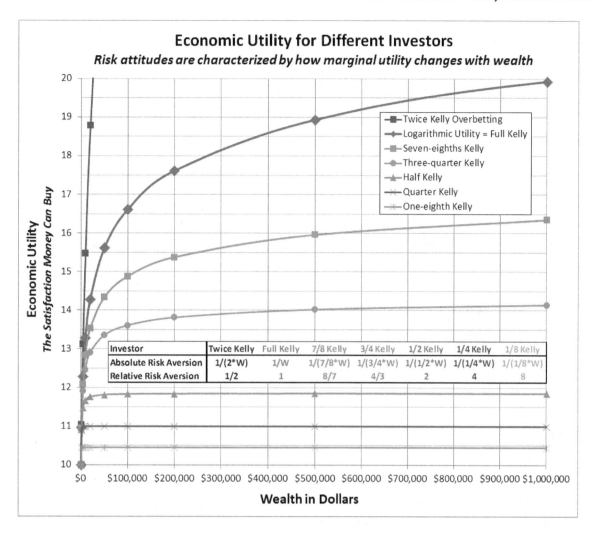

The slope and curvature of each utility function expresses the risk attitude of each investor. The tighter the curve bends as its slope falls from near vertical to near horizontal, the higher the risk aversion. The utility curve turns the corner much sharper when the risk aversion is higher. Although each investor here accepts that $1,000 wealth represents an economic utility of 10, beyond that point, the curves diverge. At one extreme, the twice Kelly over-betting investor believes that more money delivers a lot more utility. The satisfaction level of this investor soon doubles as economic utility rockets up off the chart. At the opposite extreme, the one-eighth Kelly ultra-conservative investor is quickly convinced that more money really doesn't provide much more utility or additional satisfaction at all.

When risk aversion is high, the marginal utility of additional wealth quickly approaches zero. Since additional wealth adds little utility, the risk attitude becomes "you have little to gain, so don't lose what you have". This extreme chooses the sure thing and does not gamble. When risk aversion is low, the marginal utility of additional wealth is still high. The attitude is "it pays to gamble because you have a lot to gain". This extreme makes all or nothing bets. So, different utility curves imply different risk decision behaviors.

Divide the change in marginal utility at any wealth by the marginal utility itself and you have its fractional decay rate. [Eeckhoudt, ref 40] This is better known as the absolute risk aversion, typically stated per dollar. Multiply absolute risk aversion times wealth to obtain the relative risk aversion, which is dimensionless. [Pratt, ref 41]

To the full Kelly investor, the fractional decay rate of marginal utility is inversely proportional to wealth. So, the absolute risk aversion, R_A, is 1/wealth and the relative risk aversion, R_R, is simply 1 for this investor. On the prior page, the absolute and relative risk aversion for each investor and utility curve is overlaid on the plot titled Economic Utility for Different Investors. [Ziemba & MacLean, ref 42]

If you drive to work each day, you already understand risk aversion better than you may realize. Instead of economic utility determined by wealth, consider distance traveled determined by time. The faster you go, the sooner you reach your destination. However, every obstacle you encounter along the way presents a hazard. To avert severe damage and loss of life, you must be able to stop. The assured clear distance ahead changes dynamically and limits your safe travel speed. The two-second rule was established to help avoid collisions by maintaining a safe trailing distance at any speed under ideal driving conditions. The National Safety Council actually recommends a three-second time buffer behind slower moving traffic ahead. Extra time is suggested to help offset poor lighting, bad weather, oppressive traffic, and driver impairments. Consider your vehicle's character as well. Whenever you drive, you must always decide when to brake or use the gas pedal instead.

Absolute risk aversion is how hard you press the brakes (deceleration) divided by how fast you are moving (velocity). Multiply this ratio by the time to reach the rear bumper of the next car ahead to figure relative risk aversion. A reckless driver who barely brakes, drives fast, and tailgates other cars displays little risk aversion. This green-light attitude is all offense. At the opposite extreme, a cautious driver who rides the brakes, drives slow, and trails the car ahead by several seconds shows high risk aversion. This red-light attitude is pure defense. Comedian George Carlin observed that everyone who drove slower than him was an idiot and everyone who drove faster was a maniac! Thus is the human nature of risk attitudes.

Compare the long-term record of different drivers based on their attitude and behavior. The two-second rule driver travels further over a lifetime and so, averages more miles each hour than any other driver. A four-second rule driver covers less distance in the same time because of more braking, reduced speed, and a greater buffer behind the car ahead. A one-second rule driver averages less distance each hour because mistakes are now traffic violations and serious accidents which ultimately erase gains and detour further progress. Different attitudes ultimately spawn different results.

Like the two-second driving rule, the Kelly criterion is a guideline. It tells an investor the optimum long-term fraction of wealth to risk for any investment landscape. If the payoffs and probabilities imply favorable expected returns, the Kelly fraction is high, so you invest aggressively by risking a high proportion of wealth. If expected returns are not so positive, the Kelly fraction is low, so you invest less aggressively by risking less wealth. Although the Kelly bet changes based on the investment prospects, investors often still follow their own guideline instead. ***The full Kelly investor builds the most wealth over a lifetime and averages the highest return per year.*** A fractional Kelly investor is more cautious and averages less wealth gained in the same time. The twice Kelly investor is more aggressive and averages less wealth gained because of large losses which may eventually become fatal. Although the full Kelly investor has struck a healthy, long-term balance between progress and caution, the only way to completely eliminate losses in the short-term is to not invest at all. But no pain also means no gain.

Liquidating your entire portfolio to hold nothing but cash is the investing equivalent of slamming on the brakes. Deploying all your cash to be fully invested in risky assets is like flooring the gas pedal. Most people don't typically drive this way. They should not invest this way either.

10) RECURRING CHOICES: How To Play Your Hand

Every investor invariably must decide when to brake or hit the gas instead, and how much force to use at once. Investment signals often cycle between extremes like the weather cycles between and within seasons. For example, if the Bullish Percent Index (BPI) is 0%, it has hit bottom. Widespread damage has already been done. Everything seems like a bargain. Instead of selling, the smart money here buys quality merchandise at a big discount. This tactic is like planting new crops after winter has ended. If the BPI is 100%, it has already peaked. Widespread gains abound. Everything is full price. Instead of buying, the smart money here sells merchandise at a big markup. This maneuver is like harvesting crops after summer has ended. When the BPI reads 50%, the index is neutral. But it's not clear what to do. The diagram below provides perspective for BPI changes.

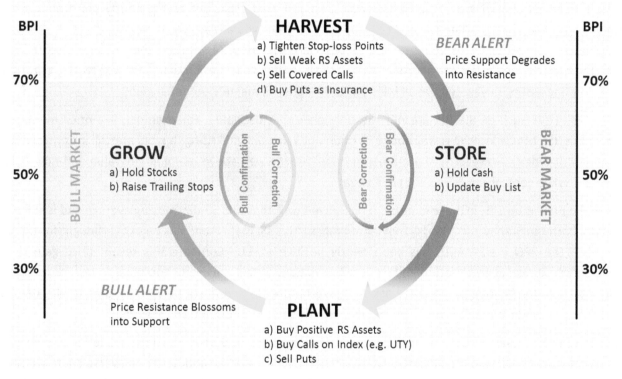

Bullish Percent Index (BPI) Cycle

BPI Point & Figure BUY signal = X column rose higher than previous one   BULLISH DEMAND

BPI Point & Figure SELL signal = O column fell lower than previous one   BEARISH SUPPLY

BPI >70% overbought, >50% Bullish; <50% Bearish, <30% oversold

BULL ALERT: BPI < 30% & then rises in new column of X's

BULL CONFIRMED: BPI P&F BUY signal & rising X column   SUMMER

BULL CORRECTION: BPI P&F BUY signal & falling O column

BEAR ALERT: BPI > 70% & then falls in new column of O's

BEAR CONFIRMED: BPI P&F SELL signal & falling O column   WINTER

BEAR CORRECTION: BPI P&F SELL signal & rising X column

Knowing just the BPI numerical value is not enough to act intelligently. It is also crucial to recognize which way and how fast it is moving. For example, if the BPI reads 72 in a column of rising X's which has climbed above the previous one on a point and figure chart, buyers now have control. This is a BPI P&F **BUY** signal. However, if the BPI reads 72 in a column of falling O's which has dropped below the previous one, sellers are now in control. This is a BPI P&F **SELL** signal. Note that the proper action in one case is exactly the opposite for the other case even though the market is oversold in both cases. This dichotomy is like a hockey player attacking on offense when his team controls the puck inside the blue line versus playing defense when the opposing team has taken possession at the same spot. Field position and possession together dictate the proper behavior, either offense or defense. The direction of motion depends on whoever has control. The BPI value indicates the field position.

10.1 STOP OR GO: Alternating Defense and Offense

You must ultimately learn to play defense as well as offense. All defensive tactics share a common purpose; they all reduce the risk of loss. The easiest way is to just hold cash, but selling poorly performing assets, tightening stop-loss points, selling covered calls (options on stock you already own), or buying puts as insurance all help mitigate potential losses. All offensive tactics share the opposite strategy; they all aim to score higher returns but typically increase costs and/or the risk of loss. The simplest approach is to hold stocks, but buying high performing assets, buying calls on an index, or selling puts all magnify potential gains.

Breadth indicators such as the BPI are not the only ones that oscillate. For example, if a price momentum indicator like RSI, MACD, or PPO is well above its midpoint value and still rising, buyers are still in control of that stock, fund, or index. However, if the momentum indicator is well above its midpoint value and now falling, sellers have taken control and driven the price down.

Suppose the price is up 12% in three months. It has stayed well above its 50-day moving average and is still rising along with both the 50-day and 200-day moving averages. The RSI is at 80 and has been overbought for the past 4 months. The PPO (i.e., MACD) has been clearly positive at +1. Compare this recent price gain to the investment's historical average return and standard deviation. If this run seems too good to last, now may not be the ideal time to play offense, increase risk, and invest more cash. It might be a better time to play defense, reduce risk, and sell or trim this investment to raise cash the moment this uptrend reverses.

Suppose the price is down 19% in four months. It has been far below its 50-day moving average for 10 weeks and is still plummeting along with the 50-day moving average. The RSI is at 20 and has been oversold a few times in the past 3 months. The PPO has been clearly negative below -2. Compare this recent price drop to the historical average return and deviation. If this run seems too bad to last, now may not be the best time to play defense, decrease risk, and sell to raise cash. It may be a better time to play offense, increase risk and use cash to buy this fundamentally sound investment as soon as the downtrend reverses.

Market sentiment indicators also cycle up and down. For example, although the VIX has a lower limit of zero and no upper limit, it has typically ranged from 12.5 to 22.5 up until the year 2020. So a VIX reading of 25 and still climbing means that investors are unusually anxious and afraid. However, if the VIX reads 25 and is falling fast, then the panic is subsiding.

Comparing an investment's price movements to its volume, market breadth, and momentum can help confirm a trend continuation or identify a reversal. An indicator confirms a price movement whenever they both move in the same direction. An indicator provides positive confirmation whenever it improves as the price increases and negative confirmation when it worsens as the price decreases. Such confirmation suggests that the price will continue moving in the same direction. An indicator and price diverge when they move in opposite directions. The divergence is positive when an indicator improves as price decreases and negative when an indicator worsens as price increases. Such divergence suggests that the price will reverse direction.

No one ever knows for sure which way, how far, and how fast an investment price will move next. But, the more signals you recognize that reinforce each other, the more likely your actions will not be at the wrong time. If all technical indicators align perfectly at the same time, they can dramatically clarify your investment decisions. The table below summarizes what that ideal alignment might look like. Each season has its own column.

STOCK MARKET CYCLE STAGES

Indicator/STAGE	STAGE 1: PLANT	STAGE 2: GROW	STAGE 3: HARVEST	STAGE 4: STORE
Signal & Season	▣→▢ SPRING	▣ SUMMER	▣→▢ AUTUMN	▢ WINTER
Price	Basing (Accumulation)	Rising ↑	Topping (Distribution)	Falling ↓
Moving Avg Price	ST MA reverses ↑	Int & LT MA reverse ↑	ST MA reverses ↓	Int & LT MA reverse ↓
Trend	Price cross ↑ SMA-50	Price > Int & LT MA	Price cross ↓ SMA-50	Price < Int & LT MA
Price Trend Lines	Price > Support Line	Breakout ↑ Resistance	Price < Resistance Line	Breakout ↓ Support
Chart Patterns	*Inverse Head & Shoulder*	*Rising Wedge*	*Head & Shoulder*	*Falling Wedge*
Abs Momentum	Price ROC ~ 0	Price ROC > 0	Price ROC ~ 0	Price ROC < 0
Momentum	MACD cross ↑ 0	MACD > 0	MACD cross ↓ 0	MACD > 0
Acceleration	MACD cross ↑ Sig Line	MACD > Signal Line	MACD cross ↓ Sig Line	MACD > Signal Line
Breadth	BPI cross ↑30 & BPI BUY	BPI > 70%	BPI cross ↓70 & BPI SELL	BPI < 30%
	% Stocks >MA: cross↑30	% Stocks >MA: > 70%	% Stocks >MA: cross↓70	% Stocks >MA: < 30%
	Hi-Lo MA10 cross ↑30	Hi-Lo Index MA10>70%	Hi-Lo MA10 cross ↓70	Hi-Lo Index MA10<30%
	A-D NYSE EMA9 cross↑0	AD NYSE EMA9 > +500	A-D NYSE EMA9 cross↓0	A-D NYSE EMA9 < -500
Price vs Indicator	POSITIVE DIVERGENCE: Price ↓ Breadth, Mom ↑	POSITIVE CONFIRMATION: Price ↑ Breadth, Mom ↑	NEGATIVE DIVERGENCE: Price ↑ Breadth, Mom ↓	NEGATIVE CONFIRMATION: Price ↓ Breadth, Mom ↓
Market Sentiment	VIX ↓	VIX < 18	VIX↑	VIX > 25 to 35
Trading Bands: Keltner Channels	Price tags Lower Band & reverses above MA	Price rides Upper Band↑	Price tags Upper Band & reverses below MA	Price rides Lower Band ↓
Risk vs Reward	Upside/Downside > 3/1	Upside/Down cross ↓ 1	Upside/Downside < 1/3	Upside/Down cross ↑ 1
Volume	Volume ↓, Lo Supply	Volume ↑, Hi Demand	Volume ↓, Lo Demand	Volume ↑, Hi Supply
Volume Indicator	CMF cross ↑ 0	CMF > 0	CMF cross ↓0	CMF < 0
Market Name	Bullish Reversal ↑	BULL Market	Bearish Reversal ↓	BEAR Market
Emotion	APATHY	GREED	SMUG COMPLACENCY	FEAR
Strategy	*DEFENSE -> OFFENSE!*	*OFFENSE*	*OFFENSE -> DEFENSE!*	*DEFENSE*
Action	*BUY*	HOLD STOCKS	*SELL*	HOLD CASH

A consensus of complementary indicators completes the following list of valid reasons to sell an investment:

1) Investment time horizon has become too short
2) Trim a position that exceeds its diversified portfolio limit
3) Business fundamentals have deteriorated
4) Investment risk is too high compared to reward
5) Total return target has been met on time or early
6) Technical indicators turn from positive to negative

The best time to sell assets is when everyone else wants them. The best time to buy assets is when nobody else wants them. Be fearful when others are greedy and greedy when others are fearful.

10.2 ONE BIT AT A TIME or ALL AT ONCE: Dollar Cost Averaging vs. Lump Sum Investment

Chapter 1 demonstrated that a series of modest investment contributions compounded over time can produce astonishing wealth. However, that original analysis presumed a constant annual investment return each and every year even though domestic and international stock markets actually fluctuate constantly. Although the historical long-term trend has been positive in the United States, short-term setbacks can still be significant. Every investor faces the same dilemma because the future is fickle. Do not miss out, but also don't lose money. Buy before the price goes up, but don't buy before the price goes down. Fortunately, as shown in the example below, investing the same amount at regular intervals disciplines an investor to buy more when the price is low and less when the price is high. This approach is known as dollar cost averaging.

Problem:
Want to buy at the low price & not at high price
Upredictable future

Strategy:
Investing the same amount at regular intervals over time disciplines investor to buy more at low price and less at high price (& overcome human emotion)

Date	Investment	Price / share	Shares
4/1/92	$240	17.125	14
7/1/92	$240	20	12
10/1/92	$240	16	15
1/1/93	$240	12.625	19
4/1/93	$240	14.125	17
7/1/93	$240	12	20
10/1/93	$240	10	24
1/1/94	$240	14.125	17
4/1/94	$240	12.625	19
7/1/94	$240	17.125	14
10/1/94	$240	16	15
1/1/95	$240	20	12
4/1/95	$240	24	10
7/1/95	$240	20	12
10/1/95	$240	26.625	9
1/1/96	$240	24	10
4/1/96	$240	26.625	9
7/1/96	$240	30	8
10/1/96	$240	24	10
1/1/97	$240	26.625	9
Totals	$4,800	17.450	275
Value now	$7,322	26.625	275

	Investment	Price / share	Shares
Low Price	$4,800	10	480
Average Price	$4,800	20	240
High Price	$4,800	30	160

Suppose you invested $240 every quarter for five years. Based on the investment price history shown by the chart above, you would have accumulated 275 shares after the 20 transactions tabulated. Since your total investment was $4800, your $17.45 average cost per share was actually lower than the $20 average price because your $240 bought more shares at low prices and less shares at high prices. Buying 480 shares for just $10 apiece in October 1993 would have been ideal, but you actually didn't have $4800 then. At best, you could have bought 168 shares for $10 apiece instead. Spending $4800 to buy 160 shares for $30 apiece in July 1996 would have been unfortunate, but you also didn't have $4800 then. At worst, you could have bought 144 shares for $30 apiece at that time. In short, dollar cost averaging can be an effective investment strategy because it puts cash to work without delay at a lower than average overall purchase price.

Dollar cost averaging clearly helps manage emotions and builds discipline, but investing a lump sum instead can sometimes be more profitable. It depends on what the future return of your specific investment will be. Of course you must already have a lump sum right now or you have no choice between alternatives.

If you don't have the full lump sum, dollar cost averaging when you buy investments means accelerating risk because the sooner you invest cash, the sooner you lose money when the price is falling. But dollar cost averaging instead of saving cash until you accumulate the lump sum also means accelerating the reward. The sooner you invest cash, the sooner you make money when the price is rising. The Chapter 1 original example showed that dollar cost averaging $100 for 463 straight months accumulated over $1 million because the price was increasing by 12% each year (1% return each month). This is far superior to safely saving $46,300 cash over the same time period. But saving and holding the cash would have been better than dollar cost averaging for any investment that did not at least break even.

If you do have the full lump sum now, dollar cost averaging when you buy investments means delaying risk because the longer you hold cash, the longer you avoid losing money when the price is falling. But dollar cost averaging when you could invest the lump sum also means delaying reward because the longer you hold cash, the longer you miss making money when the price is rising. Investing $46,300 as a lump sum that earns 12% annually for 38.6 years is much better than dollar cost averaging to invest that cash. But if the investment return was negative, the lump sum investment would have lost more value.

The more profitable strategy becomes less obvious when investment returns are mixed instead of always positive or always negative. For the $240 quarterly dollar cost averaging example, if you had invested the full $4,800 lump sum on 4/1/92 instead, you would have bought 280 shares at $17.125/share. At the $10 low price on 10/1/93, those 280 shares were worth $2,800. On that same date, the dollar cost averaging investor had $4,430 total wealth including $3,120 cash plus 121 shares valued at $1,210. But, at the $30 high price on 7/1/96, the lump sum investor held 280 shares worth $8,400. The dollar cost averaging investor had $8,160 total wealth including $480 cash plus 256 shares valued at $7,680. Finally, on 1/1/97, the lump sum investor had 280 shares worth $7,455, while the dollar cost averaging investor had 275 shares worth $7,322. So the final wealth for both investors differed by less than 2% in this case.

As Yogi Berra quipped, "The future ain't what it used to be". The same asset now at today's price is not the same deal it was last month and also a different venture than it will be next month. A large lump sum transaction can be very rewarding, but it is also quite risky. People who would never risk $500,000 on a double or nothing bet will readily risk $5 on a similar bet. Surely, no lump sum investment should exceed the Kelly fraction of wealth. Do not risk too much on any single gamble. Do not invite trouble from snakes in the grass. Compared to one big transaction, many smaller ones spread over time may diminish the reward, but also definitely reduce the risk.

Don't wait too long to buy prospective investments that grow consistently or you might miss a gain. If you have a lump sum, honor the Kelly criterion and don't pay too high a price. You can still choose to invest piecemeal. If you don't have much cash, by all means use dollar cost averaging. This strategy is ideal for accumulating investments that have volatile growth trajectories. It will help you buy low, but it can never transform a losing investment into a winner. Reinvesting all stock dividends is one easy way to apply dollar cost averaging.

Spread your investments over time (dollar cost averaging) and over different assets as well (diversification) to effectively minimize risk.

Tracking income, expenses, and investment performance every month is adequate for most long-term investors. Doing so each weekend strikes a productive balance between anticipating financial deadlines and responding to significant market events. Obsessing over personal finances each day is probably overkill except for investors who truly enjoy the challenge and have plenty of time to kill. Activity itself is not the true measure of financial success. Focus instead on establishing and maintaining long-term asset allocation targets in order to reap compounded investment returns over time. Position your portfolio to hold the right investments in advance, and the score takes care of itself.

RECOMMENDATIONS

Investment Commandments

I)   **Earn more than you spend - and invest the difference**

        Track both amounts to be sure. Spending more than you earn is ultimately financial suicide.

II)   **Never invest money you can't soon afford to lose**

        Do not risk food, clothing, rent, mortgage, transportation, taxes, or medical care funds

III)   **Match each investment to its time horizon**

        Your best investment always depends on how long you can wait for its return

IV)   **Emphasize asset allocation for long-term investment success**

        Individual stock selection and market-timing are ultimately secondary considerations

V)   **Diversify your investment assets**

        A diversified portfolio promotes investment success like a well-balanced diet promotes health

VI)   **Spread your investment transactions over time**

        Do not risk too much on any single gamble. Apply dollar cost averaging to your advantage.

VII)   **Rely on investment statistics instead of your emotions**

        Use the historical return & standard deviation to find viable prospects and manage transactions

VIII)   **Avoid losses first**

        Always quantify and limit how much you could lose before you consider your potential gain

IX)   **Invest in growth as confirmed by your research**

        BEFORE you invest, justify why each prospect's steady growth history will continue in the future

X)   **Don't overpay based on fundamental metrics**

        Compare investment P/E ratios to decide today's proper value for future prospective earnings

XI)   **Always use growth ratios to measure investment returns**

        Maximize the geometric mean investment return to build the most wealth in the least time

XII)   **Leverage technical indicators**

        Cross check independent signals to establish historical perspective and anticipate what lies ahead

XIII)   **Never establish a position without an exit strategy**

        Obey your stop loss points to sell losers. Trim fast growing winners to rebalance your portfolio.

XIV)   **Stick to your game plan. Stay focused, consistent, and disciplined.**

        It is more important to be decisive than to be correct every time.

APPENDICES

APPENDIX A: DISCRETE COMPOUND INTEREST FACTORS

Single Payment

Compound Amount Factor- Symbol [F/P, i%, n]

Converts a single present payment, P, to a future value, F

$$F = P [(1 + i)^n] \qquad (1)$$

Present Worth Factor - Symbol [P/F, i%, n]

Converts a single future payment, F, to a present value, P

$$P = F / [(1 + i)^n] \qquad (2)$$

Uniform Series

Compound Amount Factor - Symbol [F/A, i%, n]

Converts a uniform payment amount, A, to a future value, F

$$F = A \{ [(1 + i)^n - 1] / i \} \qquad (3)$$

Sinking Fund Factor - Symbol [A/F, i%, n]

Converts a future value, F, to a uniform payment amount, A

$$A = F \{ i / [(1 + i)^n - 1] \} \qquad (4)$$

Present Worth Factor - Symbol [P/A, i%, n]

Converts a uniform payment amount, A, to a present value, P

$$P = A \{ [(1 + i)^n - 1] / [i (1 + i)^n] \} \qquad (5)$$

Capital Recovery Factor - Symbol [A/P, i%, n]

Converts a present value, P, to a uniform payment amount, A

$$A = P \{ [i (1 + i)^n] / [(1 + i)^n - 1] \} \qquad (6)$$

where

P = single payment today

F = single future payment

A = uniform payment amount per period (annuity)

i = interest rate per period

n = number of periods

INVESTING ON YOUR OWN TWO WHEELS

Here are 3 college savings calculation examples using the Compound Amount Factor and Present Worth Factor. The idea is to save and invest enough each year to meet anticipated college expenses.

A = $1,000 / yr   **Case 1 Inputs**
i = 10% / yr
n = 18 yrs

F = $45,559   **Case 1 Results**
P = $8,201
A * n = $1,000 / yr * 18 yrs = $18,000

A = $2,000 / yr   **Case 2 Inputs**
i = 10% / yr
n = 18 yrs

F = $91,198   **Case 2 Results**
P = $16,403
A * n = $2,000 / yr * 18 yrs = $36,000

A = $5,000 / yr   **Case 3 Inputs**
i = 10% / yr
n = 18 yrs

F = $227,996   **Case 3 Results**
P = $41,007
A * n = $5,000 / yr * 18 yrs = $90,000

Total estimated 4-yr cost for Kent State today, 8/25/16: P = $138,899

After 18 years, we still anticipate a shortage. Thank goodness for college student financial aid!

APPENDIX B: HISTORICAL DISTRIBUTION OF S&P 500 ROLLING RETURNS

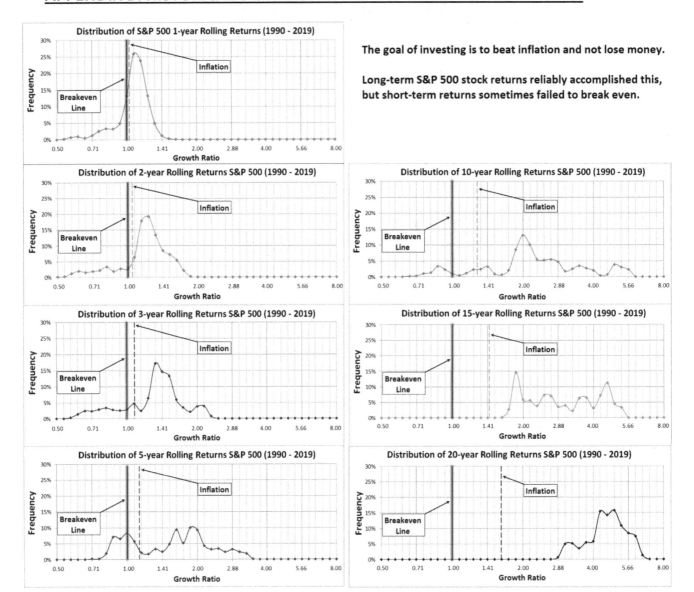

The goal of investing is to beat inflation and not lose money.

Long-term S&P 500 stock returns reliably accomplished this, but short-term returns sometimes failed to break even.

APPENDIX C: KELLY FRACTION FOR WIN OR LOSE BET WITH EVEN MONEY ODDS

Expected value of wealth, V_N, for all or nothing bet each time (initial wealth, V_0):

$$\langle V_N \rangle = V_0 \, (2p)^N$$

Value of wealth after N bets for fractional bet each time:

$$V_N = V_0 \, (1+f)^W \, (1-f)^L$$

f = fraction of total wealth bet, $0 \le f \le 1$ W = wins, $0 \le W \le N$

p = probability of winning, $0 \le p \le 1$ L = losses, $0 \le L \le N$

q = probability of losing, $0 \le q \le 1$ N = total bets, N = W + L

Long-term geometric growth rate, G

$$G = \lim_{N \to \infty} \left[\log_2 \left(\frac{V_N}{V_0} \right)^{1/N} \right]$$

$$G = \lim_{N \to \infty} \left[\frac{W}{N} \log_2(1+f) + \frac{L}{N} \log_2(1-f) \right]$$

$$G = p \, \log_2(1+f) + q \, \log_2(1-f)$$

At maximum geometric growth rate, G, with respect to fraction bet, f

$$\frac{dG}{df} = 0 = \frac{d}{df} \left[p \, \log_2(1+f) + q \, \log_2(1-f) \right]$$

$$\frac{dG}{df} = 0 = p \, \frac{1}{(1+f)} - q \, \frac{1}{(1-f)} = p \, (1-f) - q \, (1+f)$$

$$p - q = f \, (p+q) \quad \text{Since } p + q = 1, \quad \boxed{f = p - q}$$

Check: maximum, minimum, or inflection point? - *MAXIMUM confirmed:*

$$\frac{d^2G}{df^2} = \frac{d}{df} \left[p \, \frac{1}{(1+f)} - q \, \frac{1}{(1-f)} \right]$$

$$\frac{d^2G}{df^2} = - \frac{p}{(1+f)^2} - \frac{q}{(1-f)^2} \qquad \text{So,} \quad \frac{d^2G}{df^2} < 0 \quad \text{Always}$$

This expression is always negative since p, q, and f are always between 0 and 1.

So, for the highest growth rate, set the bet size, f, equal to the winning edge, $p - q$

REFERENCES

1) Riggs, James L, <u>Essentials of Engineering Economics</u>, McGraw-Hill, New York, 1982.

2) Goleman, Daniel, <u>Emotional Intelligence</u>, Bantam Books, New York, 1995.

3) Dalbar, <u>Quantitative Analysis of Investor Behavior</u>, Marlborough, MA, 2018.

4) Wilson, S.S. "Bicycle Technology", Scientific American, Vol. 228, No. 3, March 1973, pp. 81-91.

5) https://www.basketball-reference.com/leagues/NBA_stats.html, 2019.

6) Mather, Victor, "How the NBA 3-Point Shot Went From Gimmick to Game Changer", The NY Times, 1/20/2016

7) Schiller, Robert, https://www.multpl.com/3-month-treasury-rate   AND   /10-year-treasury-rate, Dec 2020.

8) Federal Reserve Econ Data, Moody's Baa Corp Bond Yield, https://fred.stlouisfed.org/series/DBAA#, Dec 2020

9) Yahoo! Finance, S&P 500 Total Return Index (^SP500TR)   AND   S&P SmallCap 600 Index (^SML), https://finance.yahoo.com, Dec 2020.

10) <u>Value Line Investment Survey</u>, Alphabet Inc., Value Line Publishing Inc., New York, Nov 6, 2020. https://www.valueline.com/

11) <u>Morningstar, Inc.</u>, Vanguard S&P 500 Index Fund, Chicago, Sept 30, 2020. https://www.morningstar.com/

12) Rodgers, Rick, <u>The New Three-Legged Stool</u>, John Wiley & Sons, Hoboken, New Jersey, 2009.

13) https://en.wikipedia.org/wiki/Unit_price_information_in_supermarkets, 2019.

14) Lynch, Peter, <u>Beating the Street</u>, Fireside Books/Simon & Schuster, New York, 1993.

15) Lowenstein, Roger, "Two Forces Drive the Stock-Market Engine", Intrinsic Value, The Wall St Journal, 30 November 1995.

16) Schiller, Robert, S&P 500 earnings yield, 30-year T-bond, & inflation, http://www.multpl.com, June 2018.

17) Hagstrom, Robert, <u>The Warren Buffett Way</u>, 2nd edition, John Wiley & Sons, New York, 2005.

18) McLane, H.J., <u>NAIC Investors Manual</u>, 16th ed., National Association of Investors Corporation, January, 1994.

19) Nyaradi, John, <u>Super Sectors</u>, John Wiley & Sons, Hoboken, New Jersey, 2010.

20) https://en.wikipedia.org/wiki/Eurozone, 2020.

21) Kloepfer, Jay, "Callan Periodic Table of Investment Returns", https://www.callan.com, 2019.

22) https:// en.wikipedia.org/wiki/Modern_portfolio_theory, (Mean-Variance Analysis) - Diversification, 2020.

23) Tornqvist, L, Vartia, P, & Vartia, Y, "How Should Relative Changes Be Measured?", Keskusteluaiheita Discussion papers, Research Institute Of The Finnish Economy, No 68, 11/9/1980.

24) Dorsey, TJ, <u>Point & Figure Charting</u>, 2nd edition, John Wiley & Sons, New Jersey, 2001.

25) Graham, Benjamin, <u>The Intelligent Investor</u>, Harper & Row, New York, 1973.

26) Appel, Gerald, <u>Technical Analysis: Power Tools for Active Investors</u>, Prentice Hall, New Jersey, 2005.

27) Haurlan, Peter, <u>Measuring Trend Values</u>, Trade Levels, Inc., La Canada, CA, 1968.

---

28) Couling, Anna, <u>Volume Price Analysis</u>, CreateSpace Independent Publishing Platform, 2013.

29) VIX White Paper, Chicago Board Options Exchange (CBOE), 2018.

30) CNN Money Fear & Greed Index, https://money.cnn.com/data/fear-and-greed, January 18, 2019.

31) Stearns, Stephen, "Daniel Bernoulli (1738): evolution and economics under risk", Journal of Biosciences, volume 25(3), 2000, pp 221–228.

32) Kelly, J.L., "A New Interpretation of Information Rate", Bell System Technical Journal, Vol. 35, July, 1956, pp. 917-926.

33) Ziemba, W.T., "Understanding the Kelly Capital Growth Investment Strategy", Alternative Investment Analyst Review, Quarter 3, 2016, pp 49-55.

34) MacLean,L.C., E.O. Thorp, Y. Zhao, & W.T. Ziemba, "How does the Fortune's Formula-Kelly capital growth model perform?", Journal of Portfolio Management ,37(4), July 2011.

35) Siegel, Jeremy, Stocks for the Long Run, 3rd edition, McGraw-Hill, New York, June 2002.

36) https://en.wikipedia.org/wiki/Risk_aversion, 2019.

37) Forelle, Charles "Why Game Shows Have Economists Glued To Their TVs", The Wall St Journal, 1/12/ 2006.

38) Bernoulli, Daniel, "Exposition of a New Theory on the Measurement of Risk", Econometrica, 22(1), January, 1954, pp 23-36. (English translation of original 1738 Latin publication)

39) Cramton, Peter, Risk Theory, Economics 300, http://cramton.umd.edu/econ300/13-risk-theory.pdf, University of Maryland, 2014.

40) Eeckhoudt, Gollier, & Schlesinger, <u>Economic and Financial Decisions under Risk</u>, Chapter 1 - "Risk Aversion", Princeton, New Jersey, 2005, pp 1-25.

41) Pratt, J.W., "Risk Aversion in the Small and in the Large", Econometrica, 32(1-2), Jan - Apr, 1964, pp 123-136.

42) Ziemba, W.T. & L.C. MacLean, "Using the Kelly Criterion for Investing", <u>Stochastic Optimization Methods in Finance and Energy</u>, Chapter 1, Springer, New York, 2011.

43) Anspach, Dana, <u>Control Your Retirement Destiny</u>, Apress, 2013.

44) Armstrong, Frank, <u>Investment Strategies for the 21st Century</u>, GNN Personal Finance Center, 1995.

45) Bogle, John, <u>Bogle on Mutual Funds: New Perspectives for the Intelligent Investor</u>, Dell Publishing, NY, 1994.

46) Brown, Robert Goodell, <u>Smoothing, Forecasting and Prediction of Discrete Time Series</u>, Prentice-Hall Inc., Englewood Cliffs, NJ, 1963, pp 97-109.

47) Dormeier, Buff, <u>Investing with Volume Analysis</u>, FT Press, New Jersey, 2011, pp 223-225.

48) Malkiel, Burton, <u>A Random Walk Down Walk Street</u>, Norton, New York, 1990.

49) Markowitz, Harry, <u>Portfolio Selection: Efficient Diversification of Investments</u>, Yale University Press, 1959.

50) Wilson, Shalett, Hunt, Edwards, et al., "Annual Update of GIC Capital Market Assumptions", Morgan Stanley Graystone Global Investment Committee, April, 2020.

INDEX

ABOUT THE AUTHOR

J. Lawrence Bixby has been an avid individual investor for over 25 years. His curiosity about fundamental and technical investment topics stems naturally from an academic background that includes engineering economics and applied numerical methods. Mr. Bixby earned his undergraduate degree from Cornell University and his graduate degree from The University of California at Berkeley. He has been a licensed engineer since 1988.

He later served as family fiduciary for over 12 years following the death of his father. After funding annual expenses throughout the remainder of his mother's life, the investments he managed also realized gains upon final distribution. He taught investment classes in metropolitan Chicago for 6 years as well to help empower other individual investors to select growth stocks at reasonable prices.

While his investments are working hard, he often enjoys cycling, social dancing, and hiking alpine trails with family and friends.

CPSIA information can be obtained
at www.ICGtesting.com
Printed in the USA
BVHW011720150421
605033BV00014B/1276